I0569843

ANGER MANAGEMENT FOR PARENTS MADE SIMPLE

SUCCESSFUL STRATEGIES FOR STRESSED PARENTS
TO IDENTIFY TRIGGERS, STAY CALM, AND RAISE
CONFIDENT, EMOTIONALLY HEALTHY CHILDREN

JULIETTE SKYE

CONTENTS

INTRODUCTION

It was one of those usual hectic weekday mornings. We only had twenty minutes until the school bus arrived, and my son refused to get out of bed. The kids were going to be late for the third time this week. I accidentally burned the scrambled eggs again, setting off the smoke detector. My first grader was freaking out because she did not like the way her socks felt on her feet. The baby was screeching at the top of his lungs in his playpen with a full diaper and a snotty nose. I was frantically trying to get everyone fed and ready for the day, trying not to lose my patience.

And then it happened. My three-year-old knocked over a glass of milk, drenching her clothing (which I had painstakingly wrestled her into just ten minutes before) and leaving a ginormous puddle on the floor. I lost it. I yelled at my little girl. The expletives that escaped my tongue were so vulgar that even a sailor would blush. The chaotic whirlwind of the morning's events led me to unleash my frustrations on my precious child. The look in her wide, innocent eyes reflected a mix of shock and hurt. With one glance at her quivering lip, I was struck by an epiphany that hit me harder than any unbridled tantrum or messy room ever had. It was one of those raw, unfiltered parenting moments where you're wavering between blinding rage and clarity. In that instance of emotional turmoil, I came to a profound realization: I had to make a change. My outbursts were becoming more frequent, and I often felt as if I was losing control. I needed to learn how to navigate the challenges of parenting without letting anger dictate my actions. My children deserved better. It became my mission to find a way to manage my volatile temper and react with patience and grace.

This is where this life-changing book, "Anger Management for Parents Made Simple," comes into play. It is not just another parenting guide; it's a compassionate, understanding friend who acknowledges the very real struggles all parents face. This book is specifically designed to provide you with simple and effective strategies for managing your anger and improving your relationship with your children, helping you raise emotionally healthy individuals.

What sets this guide apart is its heartbeat—empathy. It dives deeply into understanding your triggers, providing you with age-appropriate strategies for your children, including those with neurodivergent or psychological/behavioral issues. Unlike other books focusing solely on the child's behavior, this one emphasizes that your well-being is a crucial component of your family's emotional health.

The book's structure is like a roadmap for your journey. It begins with understanding the roots of your anger and foolproof strategies for managing it. It also offers techniques for effective and open communication and ways to customize them to meet your children's individual needs (plus much more). Above all, it highlights the importance of cultivating a joyful, loving, and supportive family environment.

My personal journey with anger management has been far from smooth. There were many times when the demands of raising children completely overwhelmed me, and I allowed myself to explode like a volcano. My poor kids were front-row witnesses to my dramatic breakdowns. I would snap at them and hurl things across the room (not at them) in unhinged fits of rage. My fuse was short, and once triggered, my anger would often take over. Sometimes, I even frightened myself because I had such difficulty calming down.

Once I recognized that I needed help and started implementing the anger management strategies taught in this book, my entire outlook and approach to parenting changed significantly. Sharing these personal insights with you isn't just about transparency; it's about showing you that transformation is entirely possible.

It is important to remember that you're not alone. Every parent has their not-so-pleasant moments, and that is absolutely normal. The challenges you face, the frustrations, and the days you lose your patience with your kids- are all part of the parenting package. But so is the potential for change. This book is your guide every step of the way. And remember, seeking help, whether it is through these pages or professional counseling, is a testament to your strength and love for your family.

The pages of this book are filled with practical advice, real-life examples, and exercises, making it more than just a good read; it's a tool for transformation. It is designed to equip you with hands-on solutions that can be immediately applied to your daily life, offering a healthier way to manage your anger and enjoy a much deeper connection with your children.

As you embark upon this journey, prepare for self-reflection, challenges, and, most importantly, the rewards of a peaceful, happy home. It might not always be easy, but I promise you, it is worth it. By the time you reach the end of this book, you will have mastered skills to manage your anger issues and created a positive home environment where every family member thrives. So, put on those walking boots and take that first step. You can do it!

1

DECODING THE SIGNALS: ANTICIPATING AND MANAGING ANGER BEFORE LOSING YOUR TEMPER

There's a moment, just before anger rears its ugly head, when your body sends out distress signals. It's a brief interlude that often goes unnoticed. Most of us are so caught up in the frenzy of our daily parenting responsibilities that we might not even recognize these signals for what they actually are: a chance to steer our reactions toward a path of calm. This chapter is dedicated to helping us uncover these subtle yet critical bodily cues. By tuning in to our physiological responses, we can learn to anticipate and manage our anger in real time, transforming our interactions with our children and everyone around us.

1.1 THE BODY'S ALARM: RECOGNIZING PHYSICAL SIGNS OF ANGER

Increased Heart Rate and Adrenaline

It starts with a quickening pulse. It feels like your heart is going to bust right out of your chest. This sudden increase can easily be mistaken for a surge of energy or excitement. However, this accelerated heartbeat is our body's primal response to perceived threats, a relic from ancient times when 'fight or flight' was necessary for daily survival. While that is useful in instances of genuine danger, this adrenaline rush often misfires in the modern world, where threats are more psychological than physical. Recognizing this bodily change as a precursor to anger is the first step toward managing it. It's like seeing dark clouds gathering on the horizon, signaling an impending storm. Just as a ship's captain would prepare their vessel for rough seas, you, too, can brace yourself to navigate the turbulent waters of anger.

Tension in Muscles

Another tell-tale sign is the tension that creeps into our muscles, particularly in our shoulders and neck. This tension is our body's way of preparing us for action, bracing us for impact or conflict. Yet, in most challenging parenting situations, this physical reaction only intensifies the stress both in ourselves and in our children. Learning to recognize and relax this muscle tension can help dissolve anger before it takes hold. Simple techniques, such as conscious relaxation or gentle stretching, can act as a release valve, easing the pressure and allowing us to handle the situation with a calmer and clearer state of mind.

Clenching of Jaw or Fists

The clenching of the jaw and fists is also a physical manifestation of the psychological battle raging within. This clenching is a sign of resistance, of a struggle to maintain control of rising frustration or anger. It's a critical moment of choice—will you tighten your grip or release and let go? Learning to notice when we clench our jaws or fists gives us a true indication of our internal state, allowing us to make better decisions about how we'll respond. Instead of clenching, we can learn to open our hands, both literally and figuratively, to the situation we're facing and approach it with openness and flexibility instead of aggression and resistance.

Breathing Becomes Rapid

Alongside these changes, our breathing patterns also start to shift. It becomes shallow and fast, which deprives us of the calming benefits of deep, steady breathing. This change is usually subtle but significant. We can help our body's natural relaxation response kick in by consciously slowing down and deepening each breath. It's a direct line to tranquility that we carry with us everywhere, a tool that can be utilized in stressful situations to dial back the intensity of our emotions.

Recognizing these physical signs of anger is like understanding the language of our own bodies. Paying close attention to the dialogue between our mind and flesh can lead us away from conflict and towards sunnier pastures. It requires practice, patience, and, most importantly, a willingness to listen and respond to our own needs and those of our children with compassion and empathy.

1.2 EMOTIONAL TIDES: IDENTIFYING FEELINGS THAT PRECEDE ANGER

In the realm of parenting, where each day brings new challenges, identifying the emotional undercurrents that lead to anger can be a game-changer. Besides the physical signs, there are layers of emotions that we often overlook that precede anger. Recognizing these feelings early on allows us to address them directly, preventing anger from escalating into a full-blown rage.

Frustration and Annoyance

Frustration and annoyance are like the constant hum of a refrigerator that often goes unnoticed until it surges into something louder and more disruptive. These emotions usually arise when our expectations are not being met or when we feel overwhelmed by the repetitive demands of our children. Our desire for peaceful, uneventful days frequently clashes with the reality of dirty laundry, non-stop bickering, and constant whining. (Parenting can be brutal at times, can't it?) Identifying these emotions requires a certain degree of introspection. We must ask ourselves what we expect and why our current reality causes us such aggravation. By acknowledging our frustrations and annoyances before they boil over, we can look for constructive solutions or adjust our expectations, paving the way for a calmer response to the inevitable conundrums of family life.

Feeling Threatened or Attacked

At times, a child's defiance or behavior can unexpectedly trigger feelings of being threatened or attacked. This emotional response usually stems from deeper insecurities or fears, such as doubts about our parenting abilities or concerns over losing authority. When we feel backed into a corner, our instinctive reaction is to come out fighting, resulting in angry outbursts. However, if we pause and try to understand that these feelings of threat are more about us than our children, we can approach these situations differently. Instead of reacting defensively, we can view these moments as prime opportunities for communication and connection, strengthening our relationship with our children rather than damaging it.

Feeling Misunderstood or Ignored

Feeling ignored or misunderstood, especially by our own children, can really sting. This pain can quickly turn into anger when we think that our efforts, explanations, or directions are being disregarded. This is especially true in today's fast-paced world, where distractions are everywhere, and the competition for our children's attention is fierce. Acknowledging these feelings allows us to get to the root of the issue—whether it's a need for better communication, setting stricter boundaries around screen time, or simply ensuring we're engaging with our children in ways that make them feel valued and cherished. By confronting these feelings head-on, we can reduce misunderstandings and feel more in tune with our children.

Impatience

Impatience is a familiar feeling for many parents. It often creeps up on us during times of stress or when the day's demands pile up and threaten to swallow us whole. It's the constant itch for things to move faster, for shoes to be found swiftly, and for bedtime routines to be followed without delay. This rush and urgency can quickly morph into anger, especially when things don't happen at our expected pace. Recognizing impatience as a sign that we need to slow down, reconsider our priorities, or simply take a deep breath can help us manage our reactions more effectively. It's about giving ourselves permission to not have everything under control every second of the day and finding value in the slower moments with our children.

By understanding these emotional signs that precede anger, we equip ourselves with the knowledge to address what truly bothers us before our tempers flare. This level of emotional awareness helps us become more attentive, responsive, and empathetic parents. It allows us to deal with the daily complexities of raising our children with an open mind and tender heart, creating an environment where both parents and children feel acknowledged, appreciated, and content.

1.3 FROM IRRITATION TO RAGE: MAPPING YOUR ANGER SPECTRUM

Anger, just like the colors of a sunset, exists on a spectrum. It can start as a faint, barely noticeable irritation and escalate to intense hues of rage, obliterating all rational thought. Understanding this spectrum is very important because it enables us to recognize the early signs of anger and intervene before we reach a point of no return. Just as a chef can learn to identify the subtle flavors in a gourmet recipe, we can learn to recognize the nuances in our anger, giving us a better chance to choose how we react.

Understanding the Anger Spectrum

You might also imagine anger as a sliding scale. At one end, there's a mild irritation—the kind you might feel when you accidentally step on a stray cracker and smash it into the freshly vacuumed carpet. It's annoying but not that big of a deal. On the other end is full-blown rage, the overwhelming, all-consuming, blazing inferno of fury that usually follows a more severe situation. Between these two extremes, there's an extensive range of emotions, each with its own intensity and impact on our behavior. Seeing anger as a spectrum helps us understand that our responses don't have to be black and white. We have the power to decide how we let these emotions guide us.

Identifying Personal Anger Levels

To navigate the spectrum effectively, we first need to understand where our personal anger levels typically reside. Self-assessment tools can be highly valuable for this. It could be as simple as keeping a daily journal to jot down instances of what made us mad and what triggered it. We can also try more structured tools, like online quizzes designed to calculate our anger responses. Over time, we can figure out our personal patterns, which show us how easily we get angry and which specific situations or behaviors light our fuse. This knowledge is powerful because it allows us to anticipate our reactions and manage them in a much healthier way.

The Escalation Process

Anger rarely jumps from zero to sixty without some kind of warning. It escalates, usually through recognizable stages. It starts with a trigger—something happens that disrupts our day and sparks our rage. Our thoughts then fuel the flames, convincing us that our anger is justified and that we have been wronged. Physical signs follow, and our bodies prepare for a fight. Finally, the emotion of anger takes over, dictating our actions. Understanding this process is crucial because it helps us pinpoint where we can intervene before we blow a gasket. We can challenge our initial thoughts, try relaxation techniques to calm ourselves or find other strategies to express our feelings in constructive ways.

Personal Patterns of Anger

Reflecting on past instances of anger can shed light on our personal patterns. Take a moment to recall the last time you became outraged. What happened just before that? What were you thinking? How did your body feel? By analyzing these moments, we can start to see our personal anger narratives—the stories we tell ourselves about why we're upset and what we should do about it. Recognizing these narratives gives us a chance to rewrite them. Maybe we can't change our triggers, but we can change our stories about them, which helps us change how we respond.

Charting our anger spectrum, recognizing our personal anger levels, understanding the escalation process, and learning our anger patterns are all vital steps toward gaining control over our emotions. It doesn't mean we should never get angry; that would be impossible because anger is a completely natural emotion.

This journey involves managing our anger in ways that enhance not only our well-being but also the well-being of our children. It requires a commitment to handling our emotions with intention and care, ensuring our responses are thoughtful and constructive.

1.4 THE RIPPLE EFFECT: HOW UNCHECKED ANGER AFFECTS YOUR FAMILY

When a parent's anger runs rampant within the walls of a home, it doesn't just evaporate into thin air. It seeps into the very essence of family life, tarnishing every interaction and shaping the emotional landscape in which children grow. Although they are often invisible at first, the ripples of uncontrolled parental anger have severe and long-lasting effects on the development and well-being of children and the overall harmony of family relationships.

Impact on Children's Emotional Development

The emotional climate of a home plays a major role in a child's emotional development. When that atmosphere is frequently stormy and riddled with unrestrained outbursts of anger, children pick up on and absorb those behaviors. They may struggle to regulate their own emotions and imitate the unmanaged anger they observe. This isn't just about copying their parent's behavior; it's about the messages children receive that teach them how emotions are handled. If the predominant message is that anger is expressed through yelling or aggression, children will likely adopt these methods as their own. This may lead to difficulties in social interactions and an increased risk of behavioral issues if children do not learn healthier ways to express their frustrations or disappointment.

Straining Family Relationships

The bond between parents and children is built on trust, understanding, and security. Repeated displays of uncontrolled anger can gradually erode these foundations, creating a gap that widens with every outburst. Children may feel anxious and fearful, constantly walking on eggshells to avoid setting off another explosion. This tension stifles open communication, leading children to withhold their thoughts or feelings, anticipating an adverse reaction. The relationship between parents can also suffer, as anger creates a barrier of resentment and misunderstanding. As these emotional distances grow, the unity of the family weakens, leaving everyone feeling isolated instead of supported.

Modeling Behavior

Children are very observant and often look up to their parents as role models for navigating life. When they see anger displayed in a harmful and destructive way, they learn to replicate these patterns. It's a form of learning that dramatically impacts and shapes their responses to challenges and conflicts outside the home and at school. On the other hand, when children see their parents handle anger in healthy and positive ways—through calm discussion, problem-solving, or taking the time to cool down—they learn valuable skills for regulating their own emotions. They realize that although anger is a natural emotion, it doesn't have to determine their actions. This role modeling of behavior is a powerful tool for teaching children about managing their feelings, offering lessons that extend far beyond childhood.

Creating a Cycle of Anger

Unchecked anger has a way of repeating itself, creating a cycle that's extremely hard to break. This cycle usually begins with a parent reacting angrily to stressors related to parenting or other pressures of life and losing their temper. Children absorb these reactions and respond by mirroring the same behaviors or acting out in other ways that challenge their parents. This provokes further anger from the parent, and the cycle continues. Breaking this cycle requires the parent's conscious effort and commitment to manage their anger issues and teach their children better ways to deal with their emotions. This might involve setting aside time for family discussions about feelings or establishing routines that help reduce daily stress. Seeking outside help can also be beneficial when the cycle feels impossible to tackle alone.

In this dynamic, every action and every word spoken in anger sends ripples throughout the family, affecting each person in ways that might not be immediately apparent. Recognizing the far-reaching impact of anger is the first step in changing the emotional climate of our home. It involves shifting from reactive to proactive, from conflict to understanding. Again, this doesn't mean eliminating anger, as that would be unrealistic and unhelpful. It's about learning to navigate the emotional tides within the family with awareness, empathy, and a commitment to change.

2

TRACING THE ROOTS OF YOUR ANGER

Imagine walking through a dense forest where the ground is cluttered with hidden roots that snag at your feet. Each step demands vigilance and careful footing to prevent you from tripping and falling on your face. In parenting, our anger can easily be compared to those roots. Understanding what causes it is more important than the stumble itself. This chapter focuses on illuminating the path, pinpointing the underlying roots of our frustrations that may trip us up, and teaches us to move forward gracefully.

2.1 THE TRIGGER TRAIL: FINDING WHAT SETS YOU OFF

Common Triggers in Parenting

All parents are familiar with those unavoidable situations that constantly test our patience. From the exasperating backtalk and drama that comes with those unpredictable tween years to the relentless pandemonium that permeates every corner of the house or the never-ending mess that magically regenerates no matter how much we clean. Day in and day out, it can be very difficult to keep our cool. The goal is to understand why these things provoke us. Recognizing these common triggers is the first step in mastering our responses to them.

- **Defiance**: It's when a simple request turns into a standoff situation, with your kid on one side and you on the other.
- **Noise**: It's the incessant soundtrack of chaos that plays from early morning until you turn that last light off at night, leaving you desperately yearning for a moment of silence.
- **Mess**: It represents a visual symbol of chaos, a stark reminder of every task left undone and how everything is piling up. It can leave you discouraged and feeling that your efforts to keep a neat home are futile.
- **Continuous bickering**: It's the non-stop squabbling between siblings, a frustrating experience that leaves you feeling overwhelmed having to play the exhausting role of a mediator.

Personal History and Triggers

Our triggers don't just stem from current situations; they are deeply intertwined with our past. The environment we were raised in significantly influences our sensitivities to certain triggers as parents. For instance, if you were raised in a chaotic, messy household, you might be overly sensitive to any kind of disorder and expect a neat and tidy home. Or if you were raised in a strict, controlling household, your child's disobedience might strike a particularly raw nerve. Unresolved childhood trauma is also a huge factor in triggering excessive anger reactions to our children's behavior. Understanding this link between our past and present can help cultivate self-compassion and provide valuable insights into how we can adapt our responses.

- **Reflect on past experiences**: Take time to think about your childhood and past experiences. How might these be influencing your reactions today?
- **Acknowledge the connection**: Recognizing that your past plays a role in your present emotions can be both liberating and enlightening.

Differences in Triggers Among Parents

What sets off one parent may hardly even register for the other. This diversity in triggers emphasizes the importance of knowing your own emotional landscape. Your partner may not be bothered by the peanut butter-smeared handprints on the wall but might feel totally undone by a child's sassiness. It's not about right or wrong; it's about understanding and respecting these differences as you navigate parenting together.

- **Open dialogue**: Having an honest conversation with your partner or co-parent about what triggers each of you can lead to greater understanding and support.

Journaling as a Tool

A journal is a powerful tool for documenting those moments, environments, and circumstances that ignite your anger. It's like being a detective in your own life, gathering evidence and clues that gradually reveal your anger patterns and specific triggers. As this diary evolves, it becomes an important asset for recognizing your triggers and devising effective strategies to address them.

- **Daily reflections**: Dedicate a few minutes each evening to reflect on your day. Write down any incidents that sparked your anger. Take note of what happened, how you felt, and how you responded.
- **Identify patterns**: Look for recurring patterns in the triggers or situations that repeatedly incite your anger. Recognizing these patterns can uncover underlying triggers that may not be immediately obvious.

Through understanding the common triggers in parenting, reflecting on our personal histories, recognizing the variations in triggers between different parents, and using journaling for insight, we can chart our unique paths. This journey doesn't just show us where we might stumble; it also provides us with a strategic map to explore our emotional landscapes with greater awareness and purpose.

2.2 STRESS AND STRAIN: HOW DAILY PRESSURES BUILD UP

Pressure can be beneficial to a certain extent; it can drive us to keep going, motivate us to achieve our goals, and promote personal growth. However, when this pressure builds excessively without any kind of outlet, it transforms into stress. This stress wears down our patience and magnifies our anger. For parents, the effects of stress exceed far beyond personal discomfort; it takes a toll on the well-being of the entire family.

Cumulative Stress Effect

Imagine your capacity for stress as a glass of water. Daily responsibilities such as meeting work deadlines, keeping the house clean, and endless parenting obligations add a few drops to the glass. On uneventful days, the water level remains steady. But on days packed with back-to-back meetings, sudden illness, or the ceaseless rivalry between siblings, the glass cannot hold another drop and spills over. This overflow is known as the "cumulative stress effect," where the build-up of daily pressures lowers our threshold for anger. Spilled juice or a missed deadline, by themselves, might be slightly annoying. But when these become the drops that make the glass overflow, it can lead to reactions that are out of proportion, driven more by the built-up stress than the events themselves.

- **Identify early warning signals**: Watch closely for the first signs of mounting stress, such as feelings of irritability, exhaustion, or anxiety. These symptoms are your warning signal to take action and attend to the stress immediately to prevent it from escalating into anger.

Balancing Work and Parenting

Keeping up with the demands of work and family responsibilities can be a monumental challenge for parents. The relentless pull between professional and parental duties can stretch our patience thin. This tug-of-war creates a perfect scenario for stress to flourish, making it easier for us to explode. We might react harshly and lash out at a co-worker for a trivial error or snap at our child for interrupting an important business call. These moments of frustration are not necessarily caused by the issues at hand but often result from the deeper challenge of balancing our dual roles. The stress of trying to fulfill our obligations both at work and at home intensifies our likelihood of anger, turning minor irritations into triggers for outbursts.

- **Set boundaries**: Establish clear boundaries between your work and personal life. This might include setting specific work hours at home and developing a ritual to mark the end of your workday, like changing from work attire into casual clothing.

Lack of Self-Care

In the rigorous barrage of daily parenting, it's easy to let self-care fall by the wayside. Yet, neglecting our well-being is like trying to drive a car on an empty tank; eventually, it will stop running. For parents, self-care isn't just a luxury; it's a necessity. It's the fuel that enables us to face the endless challenges of parenting with patience and resilience. Without taking the time to properly care for ourselves, we become more susceptible to stress, which leads to anger. Enduring a day riddled with children's constant meltdowns or unforeseen obstacles can be exhausting. Feeling over-touched, overstimulated, and underappreciated all take their toll on us mentally and physically. Facing these challenges without adequate sleep or a moment of peace can make them seem nearly impossible.

- **Integrate small self-care acts**: Integrating self-care into your daily schedule doesn't have to be time-consuming. Simple activities such as taking a quick nature walk, savoring a cup of tea in silence, or indulging in a nice hot bubble bath before bed can significantly enhance your emotional and mental health. Make it a priority to find moments throughout your day for these short but much-needed acts of self-care.

Stress Management Techniques

Since stress is an inescapable part of the parenting package, it's very important to develop effective ways to deal with it. These techniques go beyond simply helping you relieve stress; they also actively reduce the likelihood of it morphing into anger. Think of these strategies as tools in a toolkit, each one serving a special purpose to help you cope with stress more skillfully.

- **Mindful breathing**: When stress levels rise, take a moment for conscious breathing. A few deep breaths can soothe frazzled nerves and give you a chance to pause before you react.
- **Physical activity**: Regular physical activity can greatly reduce stress levels. It doesn't have to be a complete workout; even a brisk walk can help clear your mind and relieve stress.
- **Scheduled downtime**: Just as you plan work meetings and kids' activities, planning downtime for yourself is crucial. This scheduled break is a commitment to yourself and a reminder that rest is essential, not optional.
- **Seek support**: You don't have to shoulder the burden of stress alone. Reach out to friends, family, or a support group. Sharing your challenges with others can significantly lighten your emotional load.

Recognizing the influence of stress on the way we respond to challenges is a critical first step for parents striving to master their anger. Grasping how daily pressures add up, balancing work and family responsibilities, prioritizing self-care, and implementing effective stress-management strategies are all essential. These approaches help us tackle parenting challenges with greater calmness and resilience. Learning to effectively handle stress not only benefits us; it sets a positive example for our children, teaching them invaluable life skills that are necessary for developing into well-adjusted individuals.

2.3 THE LAST STRAW: WHEN MINOR ANNOYANCES CAUSE MAJOR EXPLOSIONS

Imagine this: So there you are, having somehow managed to survive another day filled with its usual challenges, from wiping pee off the toilet seat for the 98th time to helping your kid finish a forgotten science project due tomorrow. You've kept it together, handling each slight irritation with remarkable patience that feels almost heroic. You're about to give yourself a much-deserved pat on the back when something as trivial as a misplaced remote or a door left open propels you into an eruption of unrestrained fury. It's surprising how something so insignificant can spark such an intense emotional reaction in you. This phenomenon is called "the last straw." Just like "the cumulative effect," it occurs when a seemingly minor annoyance triggers an explosive reaction. This reaction isn't caused by the severity of the last incident but by the accumulation of stress from previous challenges that have built up over time.

The Concept of the Last Straw

The concept of the "last straw" develops from a series of small, seemingly insignificant irritations. Each one adds to the load, causing a gradual, unseen weight that continuously builds. On their own, these frustrations may not seem like a big deal, adding only a smidgen of stress that's easy to dismiss. Yet, when they pile up, they create a substantial burden that can catch us off guard until that one final straw (or frustration) tips the scale, triggering an outburst. It's not the straw itself that's heavy; it's the combined weight of all the previous frustrations that came before it. I like to call it "the straw that broke the camel's back."

Recognizing Signs of Mounting Frustration

Preventing a "last straw" moment depends on our ability to recognize the early warning signs of escalating frustration we discussed earlier. These signs might be physical, like tension in your shoulders or a clenched jaw, or emotional, such as feeling irritable or dreading the day ahead. You might notice your thoughts becoming increasingly negative or find yourself blowing up over things that usually wouldn't bother you. These cues hint that your tolerance is quickly decreasing, and it's time to take action. Recognizing these signs is crucial to intervene before your frustration peaks.

- **Track your mood**: Pay attention to how your mood fluctuates throughout the day. Keeping a mood journal can help you identify patterns and narrow down your triggers.
- **Listen to your body**: Your body often knows you're stressed before your mind figures it out. Watch for symptoms like headaches, stomachaches, or a general sense of anxiety. These physical cues act as early warnings, helping you handle your stress before it boils over.

Preventative Strategies

Dealing with minor annoyances as soon as they occur and managing the overall stress they cause can stop them from snowballing into severe anger. This hands-on method ensures that these issues are tackled head-on, preventing a build-up of stress that can lead to a major blow-up.

- **Prioritize**: Choose your battles. Not all annoyances are worth your time and energy. Decide which ones genuinely need your attention and which you can let slide.
- **Break tasks into smaller steps**: Overwhelming tasks are more manageable when broken down into smaller, easier steps. This can decrease frustration and help you stay calm.
- **Create routines**: Establishing routines can minimize the chaos that often leads to minor annoyances, making your day more predictable and manageable.
- **Practice saying no**: Overcommitment is a common source of stress. Be 'choosy' about what you take on to prevent unnecessary mental burnout. Don't let anyone guilt you into doing anything. Remember: No is a complete sentence.

Resetting After Reaching the Breaking Point

Even with the best of intentions, there will be times when the "last straw" breaks that poor camel's back, and we erupt into a torrent of rage. The aftermath of these outbursts can be feelings of guilt, embarrassment, or shame. However, it's important to see these instances as opportunities for self-reflection and personal growth. Resetting ourselves emotionally after an outburst is vital not only for our mental well-being but also for maintaining a stable and happy home for our children.

- **Take a time-out**: Always allow yourself permission to step away from stressful situations. Engage in activities that soothe your mind, such as a leisurely walk around the block, deep breathing exercises, or a few moments of peace. (Even if it means hiding in the bathroom to escape for a minute or two.)

- **Reflect**: Once you regain your composure, think about what led to your outburst. Identifying the sequence of annoyances that contributed to your rage can help you recognize your own warning signs in the future.
- **Apologize and explain**: If your outburst affected others, it's very important to offer an apology and explain your feelings without trying to justify your anger. Sincere apologies can repair hurt feelings and demonstrate responsible behavior for your children.
- **Plan for next time**: Consider what might help you handle your frustrations better next time. This could include adjusting your daily routine, learning new stress-reduction techniques, or simply being more vigilant about your stress levels.

Navigating daily annoyances without letting ourselves reach a breaking point requires consistent effort and dedication. It involves a carefully thought-out approach, targeted actions, and various strategies to effectively manage our stress and frustration. When we acknowledge and deal with these irritations early on, we can control our temper and prevent extreme anger reactions. Through these conscious decisions and choosing alternative responses, we build our resilience and fortify our parenting capabilities.

2.4 CUSTOMIZING YOUR CALM: PERSONAL STRATEGIES TO COUNTERACT TRIGGERS

Developing a personalized "calming toolkit" is a game-changer for managing our reactions to those inevitable triggers of raising children. Tailored to each individual, this toolkit prepares parents to not only foresee triggers but also to address them in ways that promote inner peace and family unity.

Personalized Relaxation Techniques

The quest for calm amidst the turbulence of parenting can often seem so far out of our reach. Thankfully, there are various relaxation techniques that can offer a ray of hope. Whether it's the gentle focus of yoga or the rhythmic release of a brisk jog, the goal is to find what works best for you. The quiet introspection of meditation creates a serene mental oasis, and simple breathing exercises promise a quick return to tranquility in the midst of turmoil. For some parents, creative activities such as painting, drawing, or writing provide a meaningful way to express and process emotions. Exploring these diverse techniques allows us to discover what soothes our souls and revitalizes our minds.

- **Try a variety**: Don't limit yourself to one or two techniques. Experiment with several to find which ones best suit your needs.
- **Involve the senses**: To enrich your relaxation experience, consider techniques that engage different senses, such as aromatherapy for smell or calming music for hearing.

Creating a Calm Environment

Our surroundings and the spaces in which we live play a significant role in our emotional well-being. A cluttered, unkempt home can reflect and magnify our mental state, while a calm and organized space can serve as a peaceful sanctuary. Small changes can make a big difference. Introducing elements such as soft lighting, comfortable seating areas, or a dedicated quiet corner can transform a home's atmosphere. Decorating with soothing muted colors like pale blues, greens, or earth tones promotes relaxation and tranquility. These colors are known to have a calming effect on both mind and body, helping us to reduce stress and anxiety. Plants, with their silent affirmation of life, can add balance, while decluttering can reduce visual noise, creating a more peaceful environment.

- **Designate a calm space**: Designate a specific area or corner of your home as a calming retreat. Include soft pillows and activities such as puzzles or books for silent reading. The family should recognize and respect this space as a quiet zone.
- **Incorporate nature**: Incorporating elements of nature, such as leafy plants, seashells, decorative rocks, an aquarium with colorful fish, or a trickling water fountain, can instill a peaceful and grounding atmosphere within your home.

Setting Realistic Expectations

A common source of frustration for many parents stems from the mismatch between what we expect and the realities of parenting. Rethinking our expectations—whether they're about our children's behavior, our parenting abilities, or the day-to-day dynamics of family life—can significantly reduce our triggers. It's important to understand that aiming for perfection is unrealistic. It's about learning to appreciate the beauty in the flaws and embracing the unpredictable and imperfect nature of family life. Instead of lowering our standards, we should focus on setting achievable goals that promote learning and development for our children and ourselves.

- **Focus on effort, not outcome**: Recognize and applaud the effort and progress in tasks or behavioral changes, not just the final results.

- **Embrace flexibility**: Adapt your expectations to the situation at hand, and remember that flexibility can create more favorable outcomes for everyone.

Proactive Communication

Effective, clear communication is the cornerstone in navigating through potential triggers within the family. By openly expressing our feelings, needs, wishes, and concerns before they lead to an angry outburst or conflict, we open the door for support and compassion. This involves more than just talking; it requires attentively listening and genuinely understanding each other's thoughts and feelings. This proactive approach can help us identify possible sources of tension and find ways to solve them as a family, creating an essence of teamwork and mutual respect.

- **Schedule regular check-ins**: Make time for regular family meetings to discuss upcoming events, plan activities, address any important (or not-so-important) issues, and celebrate achievements together.
- **Use "I" statements**: When discussing triggers, focus the conversation around your emotions and experiences. Use phrases like "I feel overwhelmed when..." instead of casting blame with statements such as "You always make me feel..."

Developing strategies to offset our triggers is a personal process. Centered on our desires for peace, understanding, and a deeper bond with our children, these strategies hold great power. By consistently applying them, we can find joy and a meaningful sense of fulfillment in our roles as parents. These tools, customized to suit our unique circumstances and preferences, do more than help us control our anger issues; they provide a pathway to a prosperous and enriching household filled with love and empathy.

It's important to embrace the notion that managing anger is not about suppressing it but transforming it. It's about turning our instinctive reactions into thoughtful responses and viewing each challenge as a chance for improvement and growth for ourselves and our children. Next, we'll explore breathing techniques designed to bring instant calmness. These practical, simple strategies will empower you to keep your composure through the unavoidable trials and tribulations of parenting.

3

THE QUIET STRENGTH OF BREATH

Picture this: You're knee-deep in the middle of your typical evening routine, getting ready to feed the baby, when your son dashes into the kitchen, announcing that the toilet is overflowing upstairs. The entire bathroom floor is flooded with clumps of soggy toilet paper and disgusting brown sludge, and your partner isn't home yet to help out. The baby starts wailing for his dinner as you frantically try to locate the plunger to stop the putrid tide of swamp water from further disaster, and you see the dog chowing down on the contents of the cat's litter box. You feel the tension rising, your heart pounding, and the aggravation building up. Thankfully, there's a secret weapon hidden within you —your breath. In moments like these, amidst the mayhem of daily life, the simple act of breathing can become your lifeline, offering a haven of calm to quell the storm—if only you remember to use it.

3.1 THE POWER OF BREATH: TECHNIQUES THAT WORK IN ANY SITUATION

Deep Breathing Basics

The simple act of breathing can be your saving grace when it comes to managing your anger. It might sound too easy, but that's the beauty of it. Deep breathing slows down your heart rate and lowers your blood pressure, creating a feeling of calm that washes over you right when you need it most. All you need to do is pause and take a few slow, deep breaths. Inhale through your nose, letting your chest and lower belly rise, and exhale slowly through your mouth. Just a couple of cycles of this can shift your entire mood.

Box Breathing

Imagine your breath moving around a box, stopping at each corner for a pause. That's box breathing. It's simple:

- Breathe in for four counts.
- Hold that breath for four counts.
- Exhale for four counts.
- And hold again for four counts before you breathe in again.

You can do this anywhere—while waiting for your coffee to brew or in the few moments before a meeting starts. It really comes in handy when your patience is wearing thin. The structured breathing pattern gives your mind something to focus on, pulling you back from the brink of anxiety or irritation and offering a fresh outlook on whatever challenges you might be facing.

Visualization and Breath

Combine deep breathing with visualization for a double dose of calm. Close your eyes and picture a tranquil scene, such as a beautiful tropical beach at sunset or an enchanting winter wonderland. As you breathe in, imagine drawing in the peace of this scenery. With each exhale, envision stress or anger leaving your body. It's like taking a mini-vacation right there in your kitchen or office, or wherever you are, and giving yourself a quick reset for your emotions.

Emergency Breaths

Sometimes, you need to dial down the stress *now*. That's where emergency breaths come in. This technique is all about quick, immediate relief. To do this, inhale deeply through your nose and exhale forcefully through your mouth as though you're blowing out a candle. Repeat this process 3-5 times. It's the equivalent of hitting the emergency brake on the anger train, slowing it down before a full-blown reaction crashes out.

These techniques are more than just quick fixes for anger, stress, or anxiety. They help you build a foundation of calm that can weather any storm. Whether it's the minor inconvenience of a child's selective hearing or the deeper frustration of a miscommunication, turning to your breath offers a moment of reevaluation, a chance to decide how you will react. You have the power to make that choice.

In the following sections, we'll discuss how including these breathing techniques in your daily routine can provide immediate relief in stressful situations and cultivate a lasting sense of calm and resilience.

3.2 COUNT TO TEN: BREATHING BEFORE REACTING

In the daily grind of parenting, where every day can feel like walking through a hurricane, the well-meaning advice we've all heard to "count to ten" seems so simple. Yet, it's in this simplicity that its true power is found. Merging the timeless wisdom of counting with focused breathing transforms it into a potent tool for controlling our reactions, helping us to respond thoughtfully instead of reacting in the heat of the moment. This strategy isn't about suppressing our feelings; it's about creating a moment where calm can seep in and guide our actions.

Integrating Counting with Breath

Combining the practice of counting with breathing exercises helps us stay anchored in the present moment, like a lighthouse in the fog of rising frustration. Start by inhaling deeply, filling your lungs, and slowly counting to four. Focus solely on the numbers and the sensation of each breath. Hold that breath for a moment, then exhale slowly, continuing to count. This counting isn't just a distraction; it's a way to center yourself, bringing your attention to the rhythm of your breathing and away from the source of your stress. It's like stepping out of time for a moment, allowing the immediate emotional response to pass and giving you the clarity to choose how to proceed.

Delaying Reaction

The space of time created by counting and breathing is where wisdom resides. It's a brief hiatus from the fast-paced beat of daily life that gives us a chance to assess tough situations with a clearer head. This doesn't mean we're denying our anger or frustration; it means we're aware that our first impulse may not be the most constructive. During this pause, we can ask ourselves important questions such as, "What outcome do I want from this situation?" and "Is there something that I'm missing?" or "How can I address this in a way that strengthens rather than strains the relationship?" This thoughtful contemplation, enabled by this momentary hesitation, ensures that our reactions and responses are meaningful, considerate, and in sync with our general parenting goals.

Building Patience

We've all heard the phrase "patience is a virtue." Patience, particularly in parenting, is nurtured through determination and consistent practice. Using breathing and counting as tools helps us fine-tune our ability to withstand the pressures of reacting hastily, building our tolerance, and growing our patience. It's similar to muscle training; repeated practice makes what once felt challenging attainable. Patience is especially important in our interactions with our children, whose actions, driven by exploration and curiosity, often test our limits. By demonstrating patience, we teach our children the value of taking a moment to breathe and think before we act, a lesson that will serve them well throughout childhood and beyond.

Case Studies

Consider the case of Austin, a father to two lively toddlers. One evening, during dinner time, his three-year-old decided to launch a spoonful of mashed potato across the room, splattering it all over the table and the wall. Austin felt his anger spike, a familiar heat rising. But, remembering the "count and breathe" strategy, he paused. In those few seconds, he realized that his little boy's actions were not out of defiance but a clumsy attempt at being funny. Instead of yelling, Austin explained why throwing food is not okay and suggested making silly faces with their food instead. The situation, which could have quickly escalated into a tearful catastrophe, turned into a moment of laughter and learning.

Then there's Jen, who was at her wit's end due to constant battles with her teenage daughter over screen time. Their interactions had spiraled into an endless cycle of frustration and contention. Before bringing up the subject again, Jen paused for a moment to regain her composure by taking deep breaths and counting to ten. This enabled her to control her emotions and initiate the conversation with a calm, rational demeanor, setting a positive tone. This time around, mother and daughter were able to have a more constructive chat. They discussed the rules and the reasons behind them, which led to a mutual agreement that was reasonable and respectful to both. The breathing space helped Jen approach the conversation without any pent-up anger from past arguments, allowing a more productive discussion.

These stories highlight the profound impact that counting and breathing can have on our instinctive reactions to challenges. This strategy doesn't require perfect parenting to be effective; it thrives in the messiness of real life. By adopting this approach, we can confront our daily hardships with a steadier hand and a calmer nature, turning potential disputes into priceless opportunities for deeper connections with our children.

3.3 OXYGEN OVERLOAD: ENSURING PROPER BREATHING FOR LONG-TERM CALM

Amid the hubbub of parenting, our breath can provide a steady source of calm throughout our busy days. It's easy to ignore this simple yet invaluable tool we possess for managing stress and preserving our sanity. Proper breathing helps us maintain peace and stability and guides us toward a state of lasting calm. Let's explore how making conscious breathing a part of our daily routine can transform our approach to stress and enhance our overall well-being.

Breathing for Stress Management

The connection between our breathing and our stress levels is immense. Each inhale invites freshness, possibility, and a chance to start anew, while each exhale allows us to let go of what no longer serves us, including our stress. Regular, proper breathing exercises act as a natural tranquilizer for our nervous system, dialing down our stress response and promoting a more centered, peaceful state of being. This doesn't mean our challenges cease to exist but that we're better prepared to face them with clarity and composure.

- **Start your day with a breathing exercise**, setting a tone of calm that can help ward off stress before it intensifies.
- **Use breathing as a tool** to transition between activities. Breathe deeply to complete one task before moving on to the next so that stress from previous situations doesn't infiltrate new ones.

Incorporating Breathing Exercises into Daily Routines

The beauty of breathing exercises is found in their flexibility; they can be seamlessly incorporated into our daily lives, providing an abundance of calm that is always easily within our reach.

- **Create a habit trigger**: Link your breathing exercises to a routine part of your day, such as while brewing your morning coffee, brushing your teeth, or even sitting on the toilet (why not?) This association can help ensure your practice becomes as automatic as the habit itself.

- **Breathe on the go**: Whether you're in line at the grocery store, waiting at a red light, or walking to the mailbox, these moments can be opportunities to engage in deep breathing, turning ordinary tasks into mini relaxation sessions.

Monitoring Breathing

Keeping tabs on our breathing patterns throughout the day offers valuable insights into our stress levels. We often don't notice when our breathing becomes rapid and shallow until stress has already taken hold. By periodically checking in on our breath, we can catch early signs of tension and deal with it before it intensifies.

- **Set reminders**: Use your phone or smartwatch to set recurring reminders to check in with your breath. These prompts act as a helpful nudge to take a few deep breaths and keep an eye on your stress status throughout the day.
- **Practice mindfulness**: Take a minute or two to focus solely on your breathing, observing its rhythm, depth, and the sensations it creates. This practice helps you stay grounded and enhances awareness of when your breathing patterns change due to stress.

The Role of Exercise in Improving Breathing

Physical activity stands as a pillar of stress management. It elevates our endorphin levels, uplifts our mood, and helps us feel good. It also enhances our breathing power, which in turn supports our efforts to reduce stress. Regular exercise, especially activities that challenge our cardiovascular system, boosts our lung capacity and efficiency. This improvement in physical health enhances our ability to endure stress, creating a virtuous cycle where better breathing supports better handling of life's many pressures.

- **Choose activities you enjoy**: Whether it's fast-paced walking, cycling, skiing, swimming, or dancing, the key is finding joy in movement, making it something you look forward to rather than just another mundane chore.
- **Focus on your breathing during exercise**: Be aware of your breathing patterns as you move. Aim to maintain deep, even breaths, enhancing the connection between your physical activity and your breath.
- **Incorporate yoga or Pilates**: These practices strongly emphasize the breath, offering a double benefit of physical exercise and focused breathing practice, enriching your toolkit for stress management.

By embracing proper breathing as an integral part of our daily lives, we unlock a powerful ally in our quest for calm. It's a practice that asks little of us but offers so much in return, from lowered stress levels to enhanced emotional resilience. Through a conscious effort to breathe deeply, incorporate breathing exercises into our routines, monitor our breathing patterns, and engage in physical activities that improve our breathing, we create an oasis of inner peace. This sanctuary not only shelters us from the storms of parenting but also nourishes our ability to handle them with grace and strength.

3.4 A FAMILY AFFAIR: TEACHING YOUR CHILDREN TO BREATHE THROUGH FRUSTRATION

When the concept of managing emotions through breathing becomes a common practice within the family, it changes from a solitary act of self-regulation to a shared journey toward emotional harmony. It's important for children to learn from an early age that the plethora of feelings they experience can be managed by using something as simple and accessible as their breath. This equips them with valuable coping skills and enhances the emotional bond within the family, creating a shared language of calm.

Modeling Breathing Techniques

Children have a natural tendency to mimic the behaviors and coping mechanisms they observe in their parents. When they see you turning to breathing exercises in moments of stress or frustration, they start to understand its value as a means of self-regulation. This doesn't require you to provide grand demonstrations; it's the quiet moments when they catch you taking a deep breath before reacting to muddy footprints tracked throughout the house or a broken window blind that leave a lasting impression. By allowing our children to witness us using breathing techniques to find peace amid chaos, they're more likely to turn to this practice in their own moments of turmoil.

- Let your kids know why you're taking deep breaths, in simple terms: "I'm breathing deeply to help me think clearly so I won't get upset."

Breathing Games for Kids

Introducing breathing exercises to children through games makes the learning process engaging and fun. Games like "balloon breathing," where they pretend they're filling up a balloon in their belly while inhaling and letting the air out slowly while exhaling, make the concept tangible. You can also try "bubble breathing," in which you blow through a wand to create bubbles, encouraging slow, measured breathing. These playful practices ingrain the habit of deep breathing in a manner children understand and appreciate, making it more likely they'll use these breathing techniques in times of need.

- Create a "breathing race" where you and your child see who can take the slowest breath, turning it into a fun competition.

Family Breathing Routines

Including breathing exercises in your family's daily routines normalizes the practice of using breathing for emotional regulation. It could be a few deep breaths together before dinner to help transition from the day's escapades into a quiet mealtime. Or maybe a family "breath break" during weekend activities where everyone takes a moment to breathe deeply and share how they're feeling. Establishing these routines fosters an environment where emotional wellness is a top priority, and peacefulness is not just an individual pursuit but a shared family desire.

- Start or end your day with a family breathing session, using it as a time to reconnect and set goals or express gratitude.

Through these shared practices, breathing becomes more than just a physical act; it helps build emotional resilience, improve communication, and enhance family relationships. It's a simple yet impactful way to show your children that, despite the inevitable frustrations and challenges life throws their way, they have within them the power to find peace and clarity. By breathing together, you reinforce the understanding that emotions are a shared human experience, and learning to manage them is not a solo journey but a path you walk as a family.

As we conclude this exploration of our breath's role in managing frustration and cultivating calm, it's evident that the practice extends far beyond the individual. It cements the bonds between family members, offering a strategy for navigating the complexities of emotions together. Incorporating mindful breathing exercises into our daily lives helps us realize the remarkable influence that something as simple as breathing can have on our emotional and mental well-being. It reminds us that, in challenging times, the key to finding calm lies within us, just a few deep breaths away.

Next, we'll discuss the basics of mindful parenting. We'll discover how mindfulness can improve our interactions with our children and help us create a more peaceful and nurturing family environment. This step of our journey builds on the foundation of calm we've established, guiding us in building relationships based on understanding and empathy.

4

THE EVERYDAY ZEN OF MINDFUL PARENTING

Imagine you're in a rush to pick up your kids from school, but those dang car keys are nowhere to be found. Your exhaustion from a sleepless night tending to a sick baby (who also refused to take his afternoon nap) leaves you barely able to function. You've wasted almost an hour on hold to schedule a doctor's appointment for him, only to get disconnected. As if that wasn't enough, you've just discovered bubblegum matted in your four-year-old's hair. You feel the tension mounting, your heart racing, and irritation bubbling up. It's a scenario ripe for losing your cool but also a golden opportunity to practice mindfulness. This chapter isn't about spending hours in silent meditation (who has time for that luxury?); it's about finding mindfulness in the chaotic realm of parenting, transforming potential stressors into moments of enlightenment and peace.

4.1 MINDFUL MOMENTS: INCORPORATING MINDFULNESS INTO DAILY LIFE

Defining Mindfulness

Mindfulness is about being fully present in the moment, aware of where we are and what we're doing, without being overly reactive or overwhelmed by what's happening around us. It's like watching a movie and noticing everything on the screen without getting caught up in the drama. For parents, this can be a game-changer in managing anger and stress. Practicing mindfulness can help us respond to our children with patience and understanding, even during an epic meltdown in aisle nine at the grocery store.

Simple Mindfulness Exercises

- **Savor the senses**: Pick a routine activity like washing dishes or making the bed. Focus on the sensory details: the comforting warmth of the water, the invigorating fragrance of the soap, and the smooth texture of the fabric. This focus pulls you back to the present and away from stressors.
- **Mindful listening**: Next time your child talks to you, give them your undivided attention. Notice their facial expressions, tone of voice, and emotions. Listening to fully understand rather than just responding can strengthen your bond and prevent misunderstandings.
- **Breath Focus**: Use those deep breathing techniques from the last chapter. This time, add an extra layer by paying attention to the sensation of your breath as it enters and leaves your lungs. It's a quick way to anchor yourself in the here and now.

The Importance of Routine

Making mindfulness a regular part of your day can completely transform your usual reactions to stress and anger. It's like planting flowers; they need regular loving care, but the blooms that eventually emerge can change the entire landscape of your daily existence. Try setting aside a few minutes each morning to practice mindful breathing or being fully present to savor your coffee before kicking off your day.

Mindful Parenting

Mindful parenting takes the principles of mindfulness and applies them to our daily interactions with our children. It means listening attentively to what they are saying, responding thoughtfully, and being fully engaged during the precious moments we share with them. While mindful parenting doesn't magically erase challenges, it can change how we experience them, turning moments of potential conflict into opportunities for growth—for both ourselves and our children. Here are some steps to follow to accomplish this:

- **Pause before reacting**: Feeling frustrated? Stop. Take a breath. This will give you a moment to decide how you will respond.
- **Accept without judgment**: It's important to remember that kids will be kids. Messes, tantrums, and picky eaters all come with the territory. Accepting this without judgment can reduce frustration for both you and them.
- **Connect**: Use moments of conflict or stress as opportunities to connect. Ask them what they're feeling and why. Sometimes, understanding your child's perspective is half the battle.

Mindful parenting isn't about being a perfect parent; it's about being fully present for both the good moments and the not-so-pleasant ones. It's about showing up for your kids with patience and empathy. And in those moments when mindfulness feels entirely out of reach, remember, it takes practice. Each moment is a fresh new opportunity to try again.

Incorporating mindfulness into your daily life, especially in the context of parenting, can feel like trying to find a moment of silence during a head-banging rock concert. However, the beauty of mindfulness is that it doesn't require silence or even lengthy periods of time. It simply requires dedication and practice. By starting small, focusing on your senses, or being fully present in everyday activities, mindfulness can become a practical and easily accessible tool for coping with the stresses of parenting.

Making mindfulness a regular part of our parenting routine can thoroughly change our typical responses to stress and anger. With faithful perseverance, we naturally become more peaceful and attentive parents. Mindful parenting emphasizes the importance of being thoroughly present and in tune with our children, offering them our full attention and love. This approach can turn trials and tribulations into learning opportunities for growth and connection, ultimately benefiting the entire family.

Parenting with mindfulness doesn't mean we'll achieve a perpetual state of blissful calm—let's be realistic, we're parents, not Zen masters. It means finding moments of awareness amongst the daily chaos, choosing to respond thoughtfully rather than react impulsively, and creating an environment where both parents and children genuinely feel seen, heard, and valued. By including simple mindfulness exercises in our daily routines and approaching parenting challenges with mindfulness, we can endure the highs and lows of raising our children with greater ease and fulfillment.

4.2 QUIET TIME: BUILDING A MEDITATION ROUTINE FOR BUSY PARENTS

In the daily hubbub of parenting, finding a moment of peace can seem as elusive as an uninterrupted night's sleep. Thankfully, the calming effects of meditation are not just exclusive to the solitary monk on a mountain retreat; they're also attainable for busy parents like us, even in the middle of soccer practice or running errands with a noisy carload of rambunctious kids. Let's tackle those hurdles head-on and explore how even the most time-strapped parents can seamlessly integrate meditation into their hectic daily routines, creating waves of calm that infiltrate the entire family.

Overcoming Barriers to Meditation

First, let's talk about the elephant in the room: the common roadblocks that might prevent you from sitting down and giving meditation a try. Lack of time is a major obstacle. With a schedule already bursting at the seams, carving out an extra minute or two for meditation might seem quite impossible. On top of that, there's skepticism. Can sitting quietly really make a difference in the daily frenzy of parenting? Overcoming these barriers starts with redefining what meditation can look like and recognizing its tangible benefits for you and your family.

- **Start small**: Even five minutes can make a difference. Look for brief pockets of time that already exist in your day, like during the kids' naptime or right before you start your morning.

- **Keep an open mind**: Experiment with different types of meditation to find what works for you. The variety might surprise you, from guided visualizations to simply focusing on your breath.

Meditation Techniques for Beginners

Diving into meditation doesn't mean sitting in a lotus position or doing the downward dog for hours. Here are a few beginner-friendly techniques that you can fit into any spare moments of your day:

- **Breath awareness**: This technique involves nothing more than paying attention to your breath. Inhale, notice the air filling your lungs, exhale, and feel it leaving. Ahhhhh, it's that simple.
- **Guided meditation**: Numerous apps and online resources offer guided meditation. These can be particularly helpful for beginners, providing a voice to guide you through the process.
- **Mindfulness meditation**: This is about being present in the moment. Engage fully with whatever you're doing, whether drinking your coffee or folding laundry, without worry or distraction.

Scheduling Meditation into a Busy Day

Finding time for meditation might seem as likely as climbing Mt. Everest in flip-flops, but with a bit of creativity, you can make it work. Here are some strategies to help you find those moments:

- **Wake up slightly earlier**: Setting your alarm even just 10 minutes earlier can provide a quiet space for morning meditation without cutting too much into precious sleep time.

- **Meditate with your kids**: Turn meditation into a family activity. Short, simple sessions can benefit everyone, set a positive tone for the day, or help everyone wind down before bed.
- **Use waiting times**: Turn those spare moments, like waiting for the pasta to boil or sitting in the car before picking up the kids, into opportunities for a mini meditation session.

The Ripple Effect of Meditation

When meditation becomes a part of your everyday routine, the benefits extend beyond your own well-being; they impact the entire family. Here's how:

- **Reduced stress**: Regular meditation can lower stress levels, making you more patient and less likely to snap over minor annoyances. This calmer version of you positively affects the climate of your home.
- **Improved communication**: Meditation enhances your ability to listen and be present, which may improve interactions with your partner and children and lead to more meaningful conversations.
- **Better sleep**: The relaxation that comes from meditation can improve your sleep quality, which, in turn, can make you more rested and less irritable during the day.
- **Modeling healthy habits**: When your kids see you meditating, they learn an important lesson about how to take care of their own mental well-being. You're showing them that coping strategies like meditation are normal and beneficial.

Incorporating meditation into your daily routine might seem daunting initially, especially with the countless responsibilities of parenting. However, by starting small, being flexible, and staying open to the possibilities, you can find a method of meditation that not only fits your lifestyle but also enhances it. Remember, the goal isn't to add another task to your never-ending to-do list but to create moments of peace that make your day a bit easier and much more fulfilling.

Whether it's through breath awareness, guided sessions, or mindfulness practices, the primary goal is to make meditation accessible and enjoyable, turning it into a cherished part of your daily routine instead of just another chore. Meditation can uplift and rejuvenate your spirits and bring balance and serenity to your home. This is a true accomplishment, especially in the often wild journey of parenting.

4.3 MINDFUL MODELING: DEMONSTRATING CALM BEHAVIOR FOR YOUR CHILDREN

When parents consciously demonstrate calm and mindful behavior, they lay down a path for their children to follow, one that leads to emotional awareness and resilience. It doesn't require putting on a show of perfection but letting your children see how you handle life's ups and downs with a level head and an open heart. This authentic display of mindfulness has a profound effect on how they navigate their own emotions and interactions.

Leading by Example

Children have an extraordinary ability to pick up on our cues. They watch, they absorb, and, most importantly, they mimic. So, when they see you taking a deep breath instead of flipping out or sitting quietly for a minute to gather your thoughts, it sends them a powerful message about handling emotions. Showing your kids that it's okay to feel upset but that it's important to deal with those emotions constructively is one of the most valuable lessons you can teach them.

- **React with intention**: Next time you're on the brink of a meltdown, take a noticeable deep breath and express your feelings calmly. This shows your kids that hesitating before reacting is possible and preferable.
- **Mindful apologies**: If you do slip up, apologize mindfully. Explain why you reacted the way you did and how you could have handled it better. This teaches accountability and the importance of making amends.

Learning Opportunities

Every day is filled with abundant possibilities for teaching mindfulness, often in situations we wouldn't normally consider educational. These learning opportunities are spontaneous and materialize from real-life scenarios, making them relatable and impactful for children. It could be analyzing a character's emotions in a storybook, discussing hurtful feelings after a playdate gone awry, or even exploring the sensations of the sand between your toes at the beach. These moments are perfect for talking about noticing and managing emotions, thoughts, and bodily sensations.

- **Discuss emotions openly**: Use everyday scenarios as a chance to talk to your kids about feelings. Ask them, "How would you feel if you were in that situation?" This opens a dialogue about empathy and emotional awareness.
- **Sensory walks**: Take a walk and encourage your kids to describe what they see, hear, smell, and feel. It's a fun way

to bring mindfulness into play, teaching them to notice the world around them.

Sharing Mindfulness Practices

Involving your children in your mindfulness practices can bolster your daily routine and make it a treasured family ritual. Whether it's spending a few quiet moments together before bedtime, practicing yoga on a Saturday morning, or simply sharing what you're grateful for during dinner, these experiences can create a foundation of mindfulness for your children.

- **Family breathing exercises**: Incorporate simple breathing exercises (that we learned in chapter 3) into your family routine. Meal time can be an excellent opportunity to practice breathing exercises. Before everyone begins eating, ask them to take three deep breaths together, setting a more relaxed tone.
- **Gratitude moments**: Share three things you're grateful for each day and ask your children to do the same. It can be as simple as being thankful for sunny weather or a favorite pet. This practice encourages positivity, mindfulness of the blessings in our lives, and a shared sense of appreciation.

The Impact on Children's Emotional Regulation

Children who witness and learn mindfulness from their parents develop essential emotional regulation skills that can greatly impact their well-being. They learn how to identify their feelings, understand them, and respond in healthy and productive ways. This emotional awareness allows them to endure life's challenges with resilience and empathy. It prepares them to face stress and anxiety with considerate, measured responses rather than impulsive, thoughtless ones.

- **Self-awareness**: Children start to notice and articulate their emotions and physical sensations, which is the first step in effectively managing them.
- **Problem-solving**: With mindfulness, kids learn to wait for a moment and consider various possible outcomes before reacting, which leads to better decision-making.
- **Empathy and compassion**: Understanding their own emotions helps children develop empathy and a desire to treat others with kindness and compassion.

When parents practice mindfulness, we provide our children with a template for handling their emotions with patience, stability, and thoughtful consideration. We're showing them through our actions that while we can't always control what happens around us, we can control our responses. Through mindful living, children learn to navigate their inner world and understand that emotions are like passing clouds in the endless skies of our experiences – they come and go, but they don't define us. This wisdom, imparted through the simple act of living mindfully, prepares our children with the resilience and fortitude to face the peaks and valleys of life with a steady heart and an open mind.

4.4 FROM CHAOS TO CALM: MINDFULNESS TECHNIQUES FOR THE WHOLE FAMILY

Transforming a household from a place of utter chaos to blissful calm doesn't need a miracle; it just takes a bit of mindfulness. When the entire family gets involved, mindfulness becomes more than a personal practice; it becomes a language of connection and peace shared by all. Here, we'll look at practical ways to include mindfulness into our daily family routine, making it easily accessible, engaging, and, most importantly, effective for everyone.

Family Mindfulness Exercises

Including mindfulness practices in family activities can be fun and meaningful. It's about creating moments where everyone can slow down, breathe, and reconnect with each other.

- **Nature walks**: Take walks together, with each family member taking turns pointing out something in nature they find beautiful or interesting and focusing fully on that moment.
- **Mindful eating**: Share meals where everyone takes the first few minutes to eat in silence, paying close attention to the flavors and textures of the food and the sensations of eating. Discuss your experiences afterward.

These activities don't just bring calm; they help forge lasting bonds, creating a unified state of mindfulness that can support each family member through the good times and the bad.

Mindful Communication

Open, honest communication is the cornerstone of a harmonious family life. Mindful communication takes this a step further, cultivating greater understanding and respect for one another's thoughts and feelings.

- **Active listening**: Practice attentively listening to each other without formulating a response while the other person is still speaking. Contemplate what you've heard to ensure you truly understand what they are saying.

- **Pause before speaking**: Make it a family rule for everyone to take a deep breath before responding, especially during heated moments. This small space of time can prevent misunderstandings and hurtful words.
- **Express feelings**: Create a family culture where expressing emotions is encouraged and supported. Ask everyone to use "I feel" statements to communicate their feelings clearly and respectfully.

These practices can make all the difference in how we communicate as a family, turning potential disagreements into opportunities for bringing everyone closer together.

Creating Mindful Environments

The spaces we inhabit subconsciously yet powerfully affect our mood and state of mind. A mindful environment invites peace, supports focus, eases distractions, and nurtures our well-being.

- **Clutter-free spaces**: Dedicate time each week for decluttering your home, creating an aura of calm and order. A clean, orderly space promotes an uncluttered mind.
- **Calm corners**: Designate a quiet spot in your home for meditation or relaxation. Include comfy cushions and pillows, as well as plants and calming decor.
- **Sensory objects**: Add items that engage the senses in a soothing way, such as essential oil diffusers, soft blankets, and relaxing sound or white noise machines.

A mindful home environment supports each individual's mindfulness practices. It reinforces the importance of mindfulness in our everyday lives, making it easier for every family member to find their personal moments of calm.

Mindfulness in Daily Routines

Incorporating mindfulness into the ebb and flow of daily life ensures that its benefits seamlessly intertwine with and enrich our everyday experiences.

- **Morning intentions**: Start the day by sharing intentions or goals over breakfast, focusing on how you hope to feel or what you wish to accomplish that day. Some families begin their mornings with a prayer or a few words of inspiration.
- **Mindful chores**: Turn household chores into opportunities to practice mindfulness, focusing entirely on the task at hand. This can transform mundane activities, such as doing dishes or vacuuming, into moments of meditation.
- **Bedtime reflections**: End the day with a family reflection, with each person sharing one positive experience or something they learned. This practice encourages a mindful review of the day and sets a peaceful tone for sleep.

By embracing mindfulness as an essential part of our daily routines, we not only create calm within ourselves but also enjoy a shared sense of peace and presence that benefits the entire family.

As we conclude this discussion of family mindfulness, we've learned that the journey from chaos to calm is both an individual and a collaborative endeavor. Each parent and child's practice of mindfulness enriches the family as a unit, strengthening the network of understanding, love, and peace that binds us. (Seeing the little ones participating in mindfulness can be incredibly endearing, too.) Through shared exercises, mindful communication, a nurturing environment, and the inclusion of mindfulness in our daily routines, we can maintain a spirit of calmness and support each other throughout the many trials we may face. The practices and principles outlined here are more than just techniques; they are stepping stones to a more interconnected and balanced family life.

Let's always carry the essence of mindfulness within us, allowing it to guide our interactions with our children and shape our days. This enhances our personal wellness and contributes to a family culture of empathy, compassion, and peace. This mindfulness journey we share with our loved ones is our refuge of calm in a frenzied world, leading us all toward a brighter future together.

5

CRAFTING CONVERSATIONS THAT CONNECT

Imagine a scenario where you find purple paint stains on the brand-new rug, your heirloom vase shattered by your son's indoor ball game, or your daughter's dramatic hissy fit fails to propel you into a colossal blow-up. What if these seemingly chaotic events became catalysts for deeper connection and understanding within your family? Is that even possible? It certainly can be. The secret to turning potential battles into opportunities for bonding lies in how we initiate and handle challenging conversations, especially the harder ones. In this chapter, we'll explore the core principles of successful family communication, with a special emphasis on the art of "the soft start" when facing tough conversations with our children.

5.1 THE ART OF THE SOFT START: INITIATING DIFFICULT CONVERSATIONS

When tension fills the air and emotions are running high, the way you initiate a conversation can make all the difference between finding a peaceful resolution or ending up in a heated argument with your child. Choosing a "soft start" approach can be a strategic move in these situations, as it creates a positive vibe and opens the door for a productive discussion.

Setting the Tone

A calm, non-confrontational demeanor can work wonders, like gently knocking on a child's bedroom door instead of forcefully barging in. This communicates respect and a willingness to listen to them, minimizing the likelihood of defensive reactions. Initiating conversations with "I" statements that convey your feelings rather than pointing the finger of blame makes a huge difference. For example, saying, "I feel overwhelmed when the house gets this messy and would really appreciate some help," encourages a spirit of camaraderie rather than opposition.

- **Why it works**: Maintaining a calm atmosphere keeps the emotional temperature down and encourages open conversation.
- **When to use it**: Whenever you find yourself in a position where you must confront a behavior or situation that's causing stress.

Choosing the Right Moment

Timing isn't just a critical factor in comedy; it's vital for successful communication, too. Initiating a difficult conversation when everyone's rushing out the door on a school morning or preoccupied with other distractions sets you up for failure. Choose a quiet moment, perhaps right after dinner before everyone leaves the table or during a fun family activity that isn't centered on the discussion at hand. A laid-back, relaxed setting is ideal for open and effective communication.

- **Spotting the best times**: Look for moments of calm where there are no immediate pressures or distractions.
- **How to prepare**: Before diving into the conversation, take some time to mentally prepare. Think about what you want to say and consider how you can express your message clearly and compassionately.

Expressing Needs Clearly

Clarity is your friend. The more specific you are about what you're feeling and what you need, the easier it is for your family to understand and respond constructively. Avoid using vague statements or generalizations. Instead of saying, "You never help around the house," try saying, "It's important to me that we all pitch in to keep the house clean. Can we discuss a way to divide up the chores?"

- **Benefits**: Reduces misunderstandings and focuses on finding solutions.
- **Practice**: Before starting the conversation, write down any key points you want to cover so nothing important is left out.

Role-playing Scenarios

Practice really does make perfect, and role-playing is an excellent way to prepare yourself for those complicated conversations. This technique helps you foresee potential reactions and fine-tune your strategies accordingly. Whether you're rehearsing with a friend or by yourself in front of a mirror, visualize different outcomes and consider how you might steer the discussion toward a positive resolution.

- **Scenario example**: Practice how you might talk to your teen about their recent drop in grades. Begin by acknowledging their efforts before expressing your concerns.
- **Why it helps**: This process boosts your confidence and helps you refine your approach.

By mastering the "art of the soft start," you're setting the stage for open, honest, and ultimately more productive conversations with your children. You're creating a safe space where everyone feels comfortable expressing themselves and where specific issues can be addressed with compassion and understanding. This approach doesn't just apply to parenting; it's a skill that can enrich all areas of your life, resulting in more in-depth connections and resolving conflicts in ways that fortify relationships.

Transitioning from starting conversations to engaging in them requires active listening, an essential skill we'll explore in depth next. Active listening is the bridge between expressing ourselves and genuinely understanding each other, turning conversations into pathways for meaningful connections.

5.2 ACTIVE LISTENING: TRULY HEARING YOUR CHILD

Active listening goes way beyond just hearing your child's words; it's about engaging with them and understanding exactly what they are saying on a deeper level. This involves being fully present, open-minded, and receptive to their thoughts and feelings without judgment. When we truly listen to our children, we gain valuable insights into their inner world and validate their perspectives and experiences, making them feel seen and heard.

Breaking Down the Components of Active Listening

Active listening is a comprehensive skill that includes several key elements that, when practiced together, can considerably enhance the quality of communication with your child.

- **Full attention**: Give your child your undivided attention. This means putting aside distractions, making eye contact with them, and showing openness and interest through your body language.
- **Reflecting content**: Paraphrase what your child has said to show you are trying to understand their perspective. For example, if they are stressed about a homework project, you could say, "I understand you're feeling overwhelmed by this assignment."
- **Reflecting feelings**: Acknowledge the emotions behind your child's words. If they're upset about not making the team, you could say, "It sounds like you're really disappointed about the tryouts."
- **Encouraging to elaborate**: Invite them to share more about their experience. Ask questions like, "How did that make you feel?" or use statements like, "Tell me more about that," to encourage more in-depth conversation.
- **Summarizing**: Review the main points of what your child has shared to ensure you've fully understood them and to show them the conversation was important to you.

Validating Feelings

One of the most powerful elements of active listening is validating your child's feelings. This doesn't mean you have to agree with them, but it does require you to acknowledge that their emotions are real and significant. Validation can be as simple as saying, "I can see why you'd feel that way," or "Your feelings about this are completely understandable." This affirmation can comfort them and build their self-esteem, reassuring them that their emotions are valid and they have a safe space to express them.

Avoiding Interruptions

In our eagerness to help, give advice, or share our opinions, it's easy to interrupt our children without realizing it. However, interruptions can signal to your child that their thoughts and feelings are not important or worthy of your attention. Here are a few ways to create a safe space for our kids to express themselves:

- **When someone is speaking**, pause to be sure they've finished their thoughts before jumping in with a response.
- **If you catch yourself interrupting**, quickly apologize and encourage them to continue.
- **Reinforce the importance of never interrupting when others speak**, showing respect for everyone's voice.

Practical Exercises for Improving Active Listening

Improving your active listening skills demands plenty of practice and patience. Here are a few exercises to help integrate these skills into your daily interactions:

- **Daily check-ins**: Create a routine where you spend a few minutes each day checking in with your child, asking about their day, and using active listening skills to truly engage with them.
- **Role reversal**: Have fun with role reversal exercises where your child plays the parent, and you play the child. This

can provide insights into how they perceive your listening skills and point out areas that need improvement.

- **Listening reflect back**: Practice a "reflect back" exercise where, after a conversation, you and your child take turns summarizing what the other said. This little experiment can reveal how well you listen to and understand each other.
- **Emotion identification game**: Play a game where you both share stories and try to identify the emotions involved. This can improve emotional vocabulary and empathy, essential parts of active listening.

Active listening is the epitome of effective communication with your children, helping you build a relationship based on mutual respect, compassion, and trust. By fully engaging with their thoughts and feelings, we enrich our relationships with them and empower them to confidently navigate their emotions and interactions. Through practice and perseverance, active listening can become a natural part of your parenting arsenal, vastly improving your family's communication skills.

5.3 WORDS AS TOOLS, NOT WEAPONS: CHOOSING YOUR WORDS WISELY

When it comes to communicating with our children, the words we use play a pivotal role in shaping their sense of self and their perspective toward challenges and conflicts. Just as skilled potters mold clay into beautiful works of art with their hands, we mold our children's hearts and minds with our words. Each word we say is like a gentle touch on the spinning wheel, shaping their emotional contours. Like a potter's hands, our language leaves impressions—subtle grooves that guide their growth. When we choose positive words of encouragement, we instill confidence and resilience. When we choose negative or derogatory words, we inadvertently form potential cracks that can hinder their self-worth and emotional development.

Impact of Words

It's not just what we say but how we say it that molds the impressionable young minds in our care. Our words can act as balm or blade— soothing anxieties and boosting self-esteem— or deepening wounds and planting insecurities. When we lash out at our children in frustration, using harsh or degrading language, the immediate impact might be compliance or silence. However, the lasting effects can be severely damaging, chipping away their self-esteem and casting a shadow of doubt that can dim the bright spark of their potential. Recognizing the weight of our words encourages us to use them with intention and care, ensuring that they uplift our children and nurture their spirits rather than tearing them down.

- **Embrace encouragement**: Redirect your focus from what's been done wrong to what can be done right. For example, you can say, "Next time, let's try..." instead of "You shouldn't have..."
- **Focus on the behavior, not the person**: "The way you spoke to your sister wasn't kind" is more constructive than saying, "You're being mean." This addresses the actions without labeling the child.

Positive Language

A positive shift in our language can transform the atmosphere of our home from one of contention to cooperation. There's a remarkable difference between commands barked out across the dinner table and requests made with a cheerful tone and a smile. By framing our words in a polite, upbeat manner, we can encourage conversation that invites courtesy and collaboration rather than defiance and opposition.

- **Offer choices**: Whenever possible, give options rather than commands. Asking, "Would you like to do your homework before or after dinner?" shows respect for your child's free agency.
- **Use "we" statements**: Using "we" statements promotes a sense of teamwork. You might say, "How can we solve this together?" instead of "You need to fix this."

Avoiding Labels and Accusations

Labels stick, not just the ones we meticulously peel off new purchases. The labels we attach to our children, whether shouted in raw anger or whispered in frustration, can adhere to their self-image, shaping how they see themselves and, ultimately, how they act. Telling them, "You're so lazy!" becomes a self-fulfilling prophecy, not a motivational speech. Steering clear of negative labels encourages our children to see themselves as capable of change and growth rather than confined to the box we may have unwittingly put them in.

- **Describe, don't judge**: Focus on the specifics of the situation without laying blame. "Leaving your clothes on the floor creates extra work for everyone" highlights the issue without pointing fingers or assigning fault.
- **Encourage reflection**: Prompt them to think about the impact of their actions. Asking, "How do you think your brother felt when you said that?" helps them develop empathy and self-awareness.

Case Studies

The following real-life examples shine a light on the transformative power of mindful communication.

- **Case Study: Myelie and the "Difficult" Label**- Myelie, a sassy and spirited seven-year-old, had been labeled "difficult" due to her frequent tantrums. Her parents were advised to shift their language and focus on specific behaviors. They began to praise their daughter's efforts to control her meltdowns and encourage her by saying, "We see how hard you're working to calm down when you're upset, and we're so proud of you." Over time, Myelie began to see herself not as "difficult" but as someone learning to handle big feelings, leading to fewer outbursts and greater contentment in the home.
- **Case Study: Braxton and the Power of 'Yet'**- Eight-year-old Braxton struggled with reading and began dreading it, convinced he was "bad at it." Realizing the impact of their child's negative mindset, Braxton's parents began to incorporate the word "yet" into their encouragement of him. They started saying, "We understand that reading is tough for you right now, but you just haven't mastered it yet." This simple addition of the word "yet" transformed Braxton's outlook on reading. He no longer saw it as a source of tension but as a skill he had "not yet" mastered, which motivated him to keep trying.

These stories emphasize the profound effect our words and the manner in which we communicate can have on our children's attitudes, behaviors, and beliefs. By being mindful of our language, choosing positive words, and avoiding harmful labels, we create an environment where our kids feel valued, understood, and empowered to succeed. This approach doesn't call for grand gestures or fancy strategies; it starts with the simple yet powerful act of choosing words that inspire, uplift, and encourage, lovingly guiding our children toward their fullest potential.

5.4 THE POWER OF PAUSE: THINKING BEFORE YOU SPEAK

In the incessant rush of our daily lives, especially within the madness of parenting, our words can sometimes escape our lips faster than our thoughts. The space between thinking and speaking is usually so slim that it's barely there. Yet, it's in this teensy sliver of time that the "power of pause" resides. As we have learned in previous chapters, this tool is incredibly effective; it can shift the dynamics of a conversation from escalating conflict to understanding and resolution.

The Benefits of Pausing

Pausing, even for a few seconds, can dramatically alter the course of a difficult conversation. It acts as a buffer zone, a momentary sanctuary where we can step back from the brink of impulsive reactions, gain our composure, and choose a path of calm and clarity. This brief interlude allows our emotions to settle, preventing us from speaking words in haste that we might later regret. The act of pausing is like taking a deep breath for your thoughts, giving you the chance to gather them and respond with careful consideration rather than impulsively.

- **Prevents regrettable reactions**: Quick, heated reactions often lead to regret and shame. Pausing allows you to choose meaningful responses that align with what you truly want to say.

- **Lowers emotional temperature**: When emotions flare, pausing can help cool down the intensity, making way for rational thinking and compassionate understanding.
- **Fosters understanding**: Taking a moment before responding allows you to better understand the other person's perspective, leading to more empathetic interactions.

Techniques for Pausing

Creating a habit of pausing isn't always easy, but with lots of practice, it can become a natural part of your communication toolkit. Here are some techniques to help you master the art of pausing:

- **Deep breathing**: This is your immediate go-to tool. One deep breath can provide that crucial pause and help calm your nervous system.
- **Count to ten**: An oldie but a goodie. Counting to ten (or even five) in your head offers a physical measure of pause and can help dissipate immediate emotional reactions.
- **Use a physical reminder**: Sometimes, having a tangible reminder can help. This item could be a small object you carry in your pocket or a piece of jewelry you touch to remind yourself to pause.
- **Visualize a stop sign**: When you feel the urge to respond immediately, picture a stop sign in your mind. This visual can help interrupt the instinct to react without thinking.

Reflecting Before Reacting

The space created by pausing is the perfect moment for reflection—a time to consider the most constructive response. This reflection isn't just about controlling your reactions; it's also about considering your child's needs and perspectives. Ask yourself what they are really trying to say and how they might be feeling. This helps to shift the focus from a potential power struggle to understanding and meeting your child's emotional needs.

- **Ask yourself why**: Why did your child's words or actions evoke such a strong reaction in you? Understanding your triggers allows you to respond more calmly.
- **Consider their perspective**: Try to see the situation from your child's point of view. What needs or feelings do you think they are trying to express?
- **Choose your response**: Decide how you can respond in a way that addresses the situation constructively, keeping your child's feelings and needs in mind.

Incorporating Pausing into Family Communication Norms

Making pausing a regular part of your family's communication habits can transform how you interact with each other, reducing conflicts and deepening bonds. Here are some practical ways to normalize and encourage the practice of pausing within your family:

- **Model the behavior**: Lead by example. Let your children see you using "the pause" in your conversations, both with them and with others.
- **Discuss its value**: Talk about the importance of pausing and how it can help everyone communicate better. Share instances of when pausing helped you respond in more thoughtful ways.
- **Create a family signal**: Come up with a simple hand gesture or sign that anyone can use to indicate they need a

moment to think before continuing a conversation. This can be a fun way to remind each other to use "the pause."
- **Practice together**: Use family meetings or discussions as opportunities to practice pausing with each other. This can be especially helpful in teaching younger children the value of thinking before speaking.
- **Celebrate its use**: When you or your children successfully use "the pause" in a difficult situation, point it out. This helps reinforce the value of pausing to resolve conflicts and communicating more effectively.

Remember, pausing isn't about doing nothing—it's about doing something intentional. Embracing the power of pause in your family's communication is a huge step toward creating an environment of respect, empathy, and patience. It gives us the space to think about our words and their impact, consider the feelings and needs of others, and choose responses that open doors instead of closing them. In the fast-paced rhythm of family life, "the pause" is your moment of grace—a chance to step back, take a deep breath, and move forward with confidence and clarity.

5.5 THE IMPORTANCE OF NON-VERBAL COMMUNICATION

In our daily interactions with our children, our words are just one part of the conversation. It's what we don't say that often speaks volumes, revealing our true feelings and intentions through the silent language of non-verbal cues. This multifaceted form of communication encompasses everything from the warmth of a smile to the visible tension in our shoulders. These subtle (or not-so-subtle) bodily gestures offer a rich mosaic of information about our state of mind. Learning to translate this unspoken language can greatly enhance our relationships with our little ones.

Understanding Non-verbal Cues

Our bodies are excellent storytellers, narrating our innermost thoughts and feelings without uttering a single word. Crossed arms, a furrowed brow, or an averted gaze can communicate frustration, defensiveness, or lack of interest more clearly than any words could. At the same time, a gentle tone of voice, relaxed posture, and direct eye contact convey openness, warmth, and engagement. Recognizing these cues in ourselves and our children allows us to respond not only to what is said but also to the emotions and needs that words alone may not fully express.

- **Facial expressions**: Our facial expressions are the windows to our emotions, instantly revealing feelings of joy, surprise, sadness, or anger.
- **Posture and gestures**: Our movements and how we hold our bodies can show either confidence and openness or discomfort and indifference.
- **The tone of voice**: Remember, it's not what we say but how we say it that gives away our true feelings. A softer tone can be soothing, while a sharp one can cause anxiety and hurt feelings.

Regulating Your Non-verbal Signals

Being mindful of our non-verbal communication helps us avoid sending mixed messages, unintentionally causing misunderstandings or escalating tensions. It starts with a moment of self-reflection and an awareness of our bodies and emotions, especially in stressful situations. Are we showing frustration by crossing our arms, or is our tone of voice sharper than we intended? By recognizing these signals, we can consciously adjust them to match our true intentions, ensuring we communicate warmth, patience, and openness, even when words fail us.

- **Take that breath**: Take a deep breath before responding to a situation. This will calm your mind and relax your body, diminishing any unintentional displays of tension.
- **Mind your posture**: Adopt an open posture. Be sure your arms are uncrossed, face your child directly, and lean in slightly to show you're fully engaged and paying attention.
- **Smile**: Never underestimate the power of a simple smile. It can disarm tension and express your love and affection without saying a word.

Reading Your Child's Non-verbal Cues

Children, especially the younger ones, might not always have the words to express their feelings, but their bodies usually tell their stories. Paying attention to their non-verbal cues helps us tune into their emotional state, offering insights into what they might need from us at that moment. Is their body language tense or rigid, indicating they're upset or uncomfortable? Are they avoiding eye contact, possibly feeling guilty or ashamed? By reading these signs, we can address their underlying feelings, offering our support and understanding even before they are able to verbalize their wants and needs.

- **Observe changes**: Notice any changes in your child's usual behavior or body language; it may indicate something is wrong, even if they haven't voiced it.
- **Create space**: If you sense that your child is upset, give them some physical space if needed, but be emotionally available so they know you're there whenever they're ready to talk.

- **Encourage expression**: Gently encourage your child to express their feelings, reassuring them that it's okay to show their emotions and that you're there to listen and support them.

The Role of Touch

In the realm of non-verbal communication, touch holds a special place. A hug, a pat on the back, or a reassuring hand squeeze can express love, support, and reassurance in ways that words simply cannot. Physical contact is a fundamental human need, providing comfort, security, and connection. Appropriate physical touch can be especially powerful for children; it offers tangible evidence of our love, devotion, and presence in their lives.

- **Be mindful of cues**: Pay attention to your child's reactions to touch. Respect their need for personal space and be in tune with what forms of touch they find comforting.
- **Incorporate daily**: Look for small ways to incorporate positive touch into your child's daily routines, whether it's a morning cuddle, a bedtime back rub, or a playful tickle match.
- **Match the moment**: Match the type of touch to the moment. Celebrating a good grade might call for a high-five while soothing a disappointment might require a gentle hug.

By embedding the understanding and the mindful use of non-verbal communication into the depths of our parenting, we open up new avenues of connection with our children. It's a language that transcends words, reaching straight to the soul of our relationships, where the unspoken bonds of love, compassion, and respect for one another are forged and strengthened. By tuning into these silent messages, we not only enrich our connection with our children but also teach them the invaluable skill of listening not just with our ears but with our eyes and hearts as well.

5.6 NAVIGATING DIFFICULT CONVERSATIONS WITH TEENS

Approaching Sensitive Topics

When it comes to discussing sensitive issues with our teens, diving straight into the deep end rarely yields the results we're hoping for. It's much better to wade in gently, acknowledging the discomfort without letting it steer the ship. The trick is to approach these topics indirectly or build up to them slowly. Initiating tough conversations during laid-back moments can work wonders, or while riding in the car, where it's less intimidating than a face-to-face confrontation. Use open-ended questions that invite a productive and meaningful discussion rather than a simple yes or no. "How do you feel about...?" or "What are your thoughts on...?" are excellent starters showing you value their opinions and are not just trying to lecture them.

- **Stay informed**: Prepare yourself with knowledge about the subject at hand, whether it's online safety, sex, relationships, mental health, or whatever else. This ensures you're providing accurate information and shows your teen you're taking their world seriously.
- **Share your own stories**: Sometimes, sharing a relevant experience from your own teenage years can make the topic more relatable and less awkward for them.

Maintaining Open Dialogue

Open discussion is the lifeline for healthy parent-teen relationships. It's built on mutual respect and understanding that both parties have valuable insights to offer. This doesn't mean that every conversation will be easy or comfortable, but keeping the lines of communication open, especially during hard times, is crucial. Make sure to regularly check in with them, not just about their day-to-day activities but also about their hopes, fears, and dreams. Keep these check-ins casual and non-intrusive because sometimes, listening is more important than talking.

- **React calmly to whatever they share**: Showing shock or immediate disapproval can shut down future conversations. If your teen shares something concerning, express appreciation for their honesty and take time to think before you respond.
- **Encourage them to express their thoughts and feelings**: Reassure your teen that it's safe to share absolutely anything with you, no matter how serious or uncomfortable it might be.

Respecting Teenage Autonomy

As teens transition into adulthood, their increasing desire for independence is a natural part of the process. Respecting their growing need for autonomy means acknowledging their right to privacy and personal space. It's about balancing guidance with giving them the room to make their own decisions, even if they make mistakes along the way. Involving them in decision-making, such as setting curfews or discussing consequences for certain actions, shows respect for their autonomy, helps develop critical thinking skills, and teaches responsibility.

- **Offer choices**: Whenever possible, offer your teen choices instead of giving them commands. This empowers them to make decisions and demonstrates your trust in their judgment.
- **Step back**: Allow them to lead conversations on topics that matter to them, offering guidance rather than trying to dominate the discussion.

Learning Together

Viewing difficult conversations as opportunities for mutual learning can change the entire dynamic between you and your teen. Instead of a one-way transfer of wisdom, it becomes a two-way exchange of perspectives and experiences. It's important to acknowledge that you don't have all the answers and are willing to learn and grow along with them. This humble approach can deepen your connection and encourage a spirit of teamwork in facing the inevitable challenges that life throws your way.

- **Explore topics together**: If a topic comes up that you're both unfamiliar with, make a plan to research it together and then discuss what you've learned.
- **Reflect on conversations**: After a tough talk, take some time to reflect on what went well and what could be improved. This contemplation can be done individually or together, depending on the situation.

Navigating conversations with teenagers about sensitive issues, maintaining open dialogue, respecting their growing need for autonomy, and embracing the opportunity to learn together are all integral steps in strengthening your relationship during these formative years. It's about showing up for them, not just with the intention to guide them but also to understand, listen, and learn.

This not only helps you survive the formidable adolescent years with fewer conflicts but also lays the groundwork for a solid relationship that continues long after they leave the nest.

Remember that the heart of effective communication with your children lies in your approach. Be open, respectful, and always willing to learn. These principles don't just apply to parenting but are the basis of every healthy relationship. With these strategies in hand, you're well-prepared to tackle those difficult conversations and enjoy the rich, rewarding discussions that bring you closer. Looking ahead, we'll continue to explore ways to strengthen family bonds, ensuring that as our children grow, our connection with them grows, too.

HELP OTHERS RESPOND POSITIVELY TO THE SIGNAL OF ANGER

"Sometimes, you have to get angry to get things done."

— ANG LEE

Throughout this book, we have seen how anger can result in words, actions, and emotional "explosions" that can leave us standing in a cloud of shame, regret, and fear. And if you look up thoughts and opinions on anger, you will see that nearly everything said and written about it is negative. It's almost like anger is something that automatically results in negative or irreparable consequences, something that only dwells in the hearts of fools, something that implies vengefulness and an inability to let go of past hurts. One thing that all these views ignore is the powerful catalyst that anger can be for change. Ang Lee hit the nail on the head when he expressed that anger is a signal. It can help you make powerful strides forward... so long as you know how to manage it and use it to effect necessary changes in your life.

Thus far in your reading journey, you have seen that when you have kids, anger management begins, not by focusing on them, but by focusing on you. When you recognize and label your emotions, know your triggers, and know that these thoughts do not automatically "make" you do anything, you realize that you choose how you respond to every single challenging moment. I have invited you to trace the roots of your anger and provided you with powerful strategies such as breathing and mindfulness meditation to cool down when things feel overwhelming. We have also seen how being a smart conversationalist and active listener can help tension with your kids from arising in the first place. If you find that these techniques are helping you use anger in a positive rather than a negative way, please let other parents know how you feel.

By leaving a review of this book on Amazon, you'll show new readers where they can find proven techniques to recognize, listen to, and manage anger effectively.

Thanks for your support. In the second half of this book, you will find many more effective strategies and tips to face your biggest parenting challenges.

Scan the QR code below:

6

RESOLVING CONFLICTS WITH COMPASSION

In a house teeming with the energy of kids ranging from toddlers to teens, disagreements aren't just a possibility; they're practically guaranteed. It might be a fiery debate over who gets to use the bathroom first during the morning rush or an all-out battle over which movie to watch that turns a quiet evening into a barrage of screaming, hitting, and hair-pulling. Does this sound familiar? While these moments can be incredibly trying, they also present a wealth of opportunities for growth and learning for you and your children. This is where the art of finding common ground comes into play, transforming potential discord into happy resolutions.

6.1 FINDING COMMON GROUND: STRATEGIES FOR MUTUAL UNDERSTANDING

Identifying Shared Goals

Start with identifying something that everyone agrees on. This may sound simple, and that's because it really is. Whether everyone wishes for a peaceful morning routine or wants to enjoy a fun family movie night, there's always something everyone can agree on. This shared goal is your anchor. It reminds everyone why finding a solution together is worth the effort.

- **Morning routine madness**: While you are all gathered around the breakfast table, chat with your kids about how everyone would like to start their day on a positive note. This common desire can be the stepping stone for cooperation.
- **Movie night mishaps**: Acknowledge that relaxing and having fun together is the ultimate goal. From there, devising a fair system for choosing a movie can become a team project.

Breaking Down Barriers

Overcoming communication barriers, whether they're walls of stubbornness or moats of misunderstanding, can make finding common ground feel like a quest for the Holy Grail. Fortunately, these obstacles are not insurmountable.

- **Listen actively**: This means fully concentrating on what's being said rather than just passively 'hearing' the words of the person speaking.

- **Validate feelings**: Recognizing emotions, whether it's your child's frustration about sharing or your own annoyance with the messy playroom, can open the door to understanding.

Creative Compromises

Instead of seeing compromises as losing battles, think of them as opportunities to forge new paths. It's about meeting in the middle, where everyone's needs get their own chance in the spotlight.

- **Take turns**: Whether it's deciding who does which chores or picking the next family outing, taking turns ensures everyone's choices matter.
- **Score system**: For larger families, creating a point system for completing chores and earning privileges can turn compromise into a fun and rewarding game.

Family Meetings as a Tool

Family meetings aren't just something you see in cringeworthy sitcoms. They're real-life forums where everyone can air their concerns and grievances, brainstorm solutions, and, ideally, find that coveted common ground. (We'll expand on how to have successful family meetings in chapter nine.)

- **Regularly scheduled**: Holding family meetings consistently helps remove the stigma that meetings are only called when there's trouble.
- **All voices matter**: From the tiniest to the tallest, everyone gets a turn to speak. This inclusiveness promotes a sense of belonging, self-worth, and team spirit.

Adopting these strategies into your family life allows you to turn conflict resolution from a dreaded undertaking into an opportunity for growth, understanding, and connection. It's about crafting a family culture where every adult and child feels heard, valued, and invested in the well-being of one another. This approach not only smooths over the bumps of daily living but also provides your children with vital life skills to help them navigate the outside world with empathy, creativity, and resilience.

As you continue on your parenting adventure, keep these tools on hand. Remember, the goal isn't to avoid conflict because this is reality, and that's impossible and unnecessary. The real achievement lies in how we handle these inevitable contentions- with compassion, understanding, and an unwavering commitment to finding common ground.

6.2 THE ROLE OF EMPATHY IN RESOLVING DISPUTES

Empathy is the ability to understand and share the feelings of others. It's not just a trivial skill; it's a crucial element that can diffuse tension, deepen bonds, and help us find meaningful resolutions to conflicts. Empathy is more than just a simple emotional response; it involves a conscious choice to step into another person's shoes, see the world from their eyes, and feel what they might be feeling. This act of emotional imagination is powerful and capable of transforming misunderstandings into moments of connection.

Understanding Empathy

At its core, empathy consists of two key components: emotional empathy and cognitive empathy. Emotional empathy is feeling another person's emotions as if they were your own, and cognitive empathy is understanding another person's perspective and feelings without necessarily sharing them. By combining these two types of empathy, we can work through family disputes with sensitivity and compassion, ensuring every family member feels understood and appreciated, even in the midst of disagreements.

Modeling Empathy

For parents, it's a double duty: We must embody empathy in our daily interactions and intentionally teach it to our children. This modeling starts with the simple yet profound act of listening. When a child is upset or frustrated, it's important to actively listen to their concerns without immediately jumping to solutions or judgments. This validates their feelings as important and worthy of attention. This validation is the first step in teaching empathy, showing by example how to acknowledge and respect the emotions of others.

- **React with curiosity**: When conflicts arise, approach them with a mindset of curiosity instead of correction. Asking questions like, "Can you help me understand why you're feeling this way?" provides insight into your child's perspective and demonstrates an empathetic way of problem-solving.
- **Share your feelings**: Letting your children see how you handle your emotions, including moments of vulnerability, teaches them that all feelings have value. By sharing your feelings, such as disappointment or hurt caused by a particular action or situation, you show them how to express emotions in a healthy, constructive way.

Empathy Exercises

Creating a family culture rich in empathy requires plenty of intentional practice. Here are a few exercises designed to cultivate a better understanding and appreciation of each other's thoughts and feelings:

- **Emotion charades**: This game is a playful way to explore emotions. Everyone takes turns acting out different feelings without words, while others guess the emotion. It's a fun exercise that helps children become more in tune with each other's non-verbal emotional cues.
- **Perspective-taking stories**: During family time, share stories or scenarios and discuss them from the perspectives of each character involved. This exercise teaches children to consider multiple viewpoints and understand that every story has more than one side.
- **Emotion diary**: Encourage your children to keep a diary of their emotions for a week, noting how they felt in different situations and why. Sharing these diaries in a family meeting can open up discussions about how each person perceives and experiences things differently.

Resolving Conflicts with Empathy

Empathy can turn the tide in conflict resolution by shifting the focus from winning an argument to truly understanding each other's needs and feelings. Here are some ways empathy can transform family disputes:

- **Empathetic listening in action**: Imagine a scenario where two siblings fight over whose turn it is to play a video game. Instead of immediately imposing a solution, you take the time to sit with them and listen to each child's feelings and standpoints. After you have heard both sides, you say, "It sounds like you both really enjoy this game and want a turn to play with it." This acknowledgment can soothe feelings of aggravation and light the way for a mutually agreeable resolution.

- **Finding the emotional root of the conflict**: Many times, what we fight about isn't the real issue. A quarrel about chores might really be about feeling unappreciated or overwhelmed. By recognizing the emotional undercurrents, we can uncover the real needs at play and come up with more meaningful solutions.

Empathy, with its inherent ability to promote understanding and connection, is a key ingredient in resolving family disputes. It encourages us to look beyond the surface of disagreements to the emotions and needs behind them and to find solutions that honor those feelings. By practicing empathy, we not only resolve the conflicts at hand but also strengthen our family unit, teaching our children the value of understanding and compassion in all their relationships and interactions with others.

6.3 NAVIGATING NEGOTIATIONS: SOLUTIONS THAT WORK FOR EVERYONE

In the bustling ecosystem of family life, where everyone's needs and desires constantly collide and overlap, mastering the art of negotiation can be a lifesaver. This isn't about using boardroom tactics or leveraging power; it's about building a spirit of cooperation and respect for each other.

Here, we'll examine the art of negotiation within the family, aiming to equip both parents and children with the skills needed to reach agreements that leave everyone feeling seen, heard, and valued.

Principles of Fair Negotiation

Negotiation, in its most nurturing form, is grounded in fairness and respect. It's about coming together to find solutions that everyone can live with rather than one side claiming victory. Here are the pillars that uphold fair negotiation within the family:

- **Equality**: Everyone's voice deserves equal weight, regardless of age. Children's preferences and opinions should be given the same consideration as those of grown-ups.
- **Open-mindedness**: Approach negotiations with a willingness to explore all options. Being fixated on one outcome can prevent the discovery of potentially better solutions.
- **Respect**: Even in disagreement, maintaining respect for each other's viewpoints is crucial. This means listening without interrupting and acknowledging the other person's thoughts and opinions.
- **Transparency**: Be clear about what you need and why. Hidden agendas or holding back information can lead to solutions that don't truly address everyone's needs.

By sticking to these principles for successful negotiation, families can work through conflicts with a sense of collaboration and mutual respect. This paves the way for finding resolutions that strengthen and improve relationships rather than straining them.

Teaching Negotiation Skills to Children

Teaching children proper negotiation skills does more than just smooth over sibling spats; it prepares them for life in the real world. Here's how to start:

- **Modeling negotiation**: Let them observe you negotiating in real life. Whether you're discussing dinner plans with your partner or deciding on a family activity, show them how it's done.
- **Role clarification**: Help them understand their role in negotiations. This includes expressing their needs clearly, listening to others, and being open to compromise.
- **Problem-solving together**: Involve them in solving everyday problems through negotiation. Whether it's deciding what show to watch or helping each other with chores, use these opportunities to practice negotiating skills.
- **Praise and feedback**: Acknowledge when they use negotiation skills well and offer gentle guidance when there's room for improvement.

With consistent practice and positive reinforcement, our children can develop the confidence and competence to navigate negotiations effectively, setting them up for success within the family and beyond.

Negotiation Role-Play Scenarios

Role-playing is an excellent way for children to practice negotiation skills in a safe, controlled environment. Here are a couple of scenarios to help you get started:

Scenario 1: Weekend Plans

- **Context**: One child wants to go to the zoo, another prefers swimming, and you're leaning toward a quiet day at home.
- **Objective**: Come up with a plan that incorporates everyone's interests.
- **Roles**: Each family member, including you, argues their case, then switches roles to argue another person's preference.
- **Learning point**: This scenario teaches empathy and the importance of considering others' desires in negotiation.

Scenario 2: Household Chores

- **Context**: Disagreement over who should do which chore.
- **Objective**: Assign chores in a way that feels fair to everyone.
- **Roles**: Each family member presents their preferences and dislikes and then explores creative solutions, such as trading chores or working together on the less popular ones.
- **Learning point**: This scenario highlights the value of being clear about our wants and needs and finding creative compromises to reach solutions everyone agrees on.

Role-playing not only enhances negotiation skills but also adds an element of fun into learning how to resolve conflicts, making the lessons more likely to stick.

Win-Win Solutions

The ultimate pursuit of successful family negotiations is finding solutions that address and satisfy each person's needs and wants-

otherwise known as "win-win" outcomes. Achieving this requires a shift from thinking about what we're willing to give up to exploring how everyone's desires can be met. Here are some tips to help steer discussions toward win-win solutions:

- **Focus on interests, not positions**: Dig deeper to understand why someone might want what they want. This can open up new avenues for agreement that might not be apparent initially.
- **Brainstorm together**: Encourage all family members to share their ideas, no matter how silly or odd they may seem. The more options on the table, the easier it is to find solutions everyone likes.
- **Be willing to experiment**: Not all solutions will be perfect from the start. Be open to trying out different ideas with the understanding that they can be adjusted based on how well they work for everyone.

Formulating win-win solutions is more than just a negotiation tactic; it's a way of building a framework of cooperation and support that holds the family together. Through open conversation, creative problem-solving, and a commitment to meeting everyone's needs, families can turn potential conflicts and disagreements into opportunities to uplift and sustain one another, ensuring everyone feels included and appreciated.

6.4 APOLOGY AND FORGIVENESS: HEALING AFTER THE ANGER

A genuine apology has the power to mend fences and heal wounds, acting as a salve on the sting left by harsh words or unkind deeds. When we apologize sincerely, we admit our wrongdoings, take responsibility for our behavior, and express our commitment to doing better in the future. This act of vulnerability is not a sign of weakness; it demonstrates strength, humility, and a deep respect for the feelings of others.

The Power of a Sincere Apology

A true apology involves more than just uttering the words "I'm sorry." It's a heartfelt acknowledgment that your actions hurt someone, along with an honest effort to make amends. Here are the components that make an apology effective:

- **Acknowledge the mistake**: Clearly state what you did wrong without making excuses.
- **Understand the impact**: Show that you realize how your actions affected the other person.
- **Commit to making a change**: Express your intention to avoid repeating the same mistake and discuss how you plan to prevent it from happening again.

This process not only helps heal the wounds caused by your indiscretion but also reinforces the relationship by rebuilding trust.

Teaching Children About Forgiveness

Forgiveness, much like empathy, is a skill that children learn over time, and it's crucial for parents to guide them in recognizing its importance. Teaching forgiveness involves helping children see past their immediate hurt to the bigger picture of human fallibility and the redeeming power of compassion and understanding. Here are ways to teach your children the value of forgiveness:

- **Lead by example**: Forgive others openly and discuss the process with your children, explaining why you chose to forgive and how it made you feel.
- **Discuss the benefits**: Talk about how forgiveness can free us from lingering anger and resentment, leading to happier and more peaceful lives.
- **Encourage empathy**: Help them put themselves in the other person's shoes so they can see that everyone makes mistakes and deserves a chance for redemption.

Creating a Culture of Accountability and Forgiveness in the Family

Cultivating an environment where apologies and forgiveness are encouraged and valued sets the stage for a healthy, stable, and resilient family dynamic. Here's how we can nurture this culture in our homes:

- **Normalize apologies**: Make it clear that everyone makes mistakes and that apologizing is a sign of maturity and respect.
- **Celebrate acts of forgiveness**: Recognize and praise moments when your children choose to forgive, reinforcing it as a commendable behavior.
- **Hold family discussions**: When conflicts arise, hold discussions that allow everyone involved to express their feelings, apologize if necessary, and work together to find ways to move on.

This approach not only resolves current conflicts but also teaches valuable life lessons about responsibility, empathy, and the healing power of forgiveness.

Rebuilding Trust After Conflicts

Trust, once it has been broken, takes time and effort to rebuild. Here are a few strategies that can help repair the foundation of trust and heal wounded relationships in the aftermath of conflicts:

- **Follow through on promises**: Ensure that any promises or commitments made during an apology are met. Consistency in actions speaks louder than words and is vital for rebuilding trust.
- **Be patient**: Remember that regaining trust doesn't happen overnight. Allow time for the healing process to unfold naturally.
- **Open communication**: Maintain open lines of communication, encouraging your children to share their feelings and concerns as they walk the path to forgiveness.

Although these steps may seem simple in theory, they require dedication and patience. The reward of a stronger, more trusting family bond makes the effort worthwhile.

Emphasize the Importance of Forgiving Yourself

In the journey towards cultivating forgiveness in your family, it's critical to not overlook the importance of forgiving yourself. Holding onto self-blame and guilt can be as damaging as harboring resentment towards others. Remember that being human means being imperfect. No parent on earth is without fault. (Not even the ones showing off their "flawless" lives on Instagram.) Acknowledge your mistakes, learn from them, and give yourself permission to move on. This self-compassion not only benefits your own healing but also sets a great example for your children, teaching them that it's okay to forgive themselves, too.

In the end, the dance of apology and forgiveness within a family is a delicate one, filled with steps of humility, understanding, and compassion. Through this dance, we teach our children not just to navigate the conflicts that arise within the home but also to carry these lessons into the world, spreading kindness and empathy wherever they go.

As we close this chapter on resolving conflicts with compassion, let's never forget that within the heart of every family, despite the occasional disagreements, there is a deep-seated love and a shared commitment to encouraging and supporting one another. This foundation, built on the principles of empathy, negotiation, and forgiveness, not only resolves conflicts but also brings us closer together, preparing us all for the challenges and joys that await us in our journey as a family.

7

UNLOCKING THE LANGUAGE OF EMOTIONS

Imagine that you're handed a map to a foreign land, but it's unlike any map you've ever seen. Instead of roads and landmarks, it's filled with emotions and behaviors. It's a unique guide to help you navigate the complex emotional landscape of your child. This isn't just about finding the quickest route to calming your little one's meltdown or decoding the silent treatment from your moody teen. It's about understanding the intricate terrain of feelings that drive these behaviors, allowing you to connect with your child on a deeper level. Let's explore this map and discover how empathy, active listening, and validating your children's feelings can revolutionize your parenting approach, making every interaction with your child a stepping stone toward mutual understanding and respect.

7.1 BUILDING BRIDGES: THE POWER OF TEACHING EMPATHY TO CHILDREN

Empathy as a Tool

Empathy is like a bridge. On one side, you have your child's actions or reactions, which are often perplexing or frustrating. On the other side are the emotions and needs that fuel those behaviors. Crossing this bridge requires empathy, a tool that allows you to see the world through your child's eyes. It's not just understanding the "what" of their actions but also the "why" behind them. It's about viewing your son's clenched fists not as defiance but as a manifestation of anxiety or interpreting your daughter's withdrawal not as indifference but as sadness.

- **In the moment**: When you encounter challenging behavior, pause and ask yourself, "What could my child be feeling right now?" This question helps shift your mindset, opening the door to empathy.
- **Practice perspective-taking**: During quieter moments together, talk to your child about how you think he or she might feel about various aspects of their life, from school pressures to friendships. This sharpens your empathy skills and models them for your child.

Child Development and Emotion

It's important to understand that your child's emotional world isn't one-size-fits-all; it depends on their current stage of development. A baby's cry, a toddler's tantrum, a preschooler's incessant questions, or a teenager's mood swings are all expressions of their evolving emotional landscape. Recognizing what is typical at each age and stage helps you adjust your responses and expectations.

- **For toddlers**: Their frustration often stems from the disparity between their desires and their abilities. Acknowledge their frustration by saying, "I know you want to put that puzzle together, but it's kind of tricky, isn't it?
- **For teens**: Their emotional unpredictability is partly due to the hormonal rollercoaster of adolescence. Validate their feelings without brushing them off as just a phase. You could say, "I know you're really upset about this. It's okay to feel this way."

Active Listening for Emotional Cues

Active listening is your compass in this landscape, guiding you to the core of your child's emotional state. It's more than just hearing their words; it means tuning into their tone of voice, body language, and anything that may be left unsaid. This form of listening creates a safe space where your child feels comfortable expressing their emotions, knowing they'll be heard, understood, and taken seriously.

- **Reflection**: After listening to your child, summarize what you've heard in your own words, "So, what you're saying is..."
- **Validate emotions**: Use phrases like, "That sounds very upsetting," to acknowledge their feelings.
- **Non-verbal cues**: Pay close attention to your child's sighs, eye rolls, or slumped shoulders as much as their words. These bodily clues often speak volumes about what they're feeling but might not be ready to talk about.

Validating Feelings

Your child's emotions are like raindrops falling from the sky, and your validation is the umbrella that acknowledges the rain without trying to stop the downpour. It's a powerful form of support, showing your child that it's perfectly okay to feel whatever they're feeling. This validation doesn't necessarily mean you agree with their perspective but that you accept their feelings as valid.

- **During a meltdown**: Instead of trying to fix things immediately, validate your child's feelings first. You might say, "I know you're really mad that we have to leave the park. I understand that you'd like to play longer."
- **In daily conversations**: Make it a habit to validate your child's feelings even in everyday conversations. For example, "You seem excited about the science fair," or "You sound worried about the test tomorrow."

By weaving empathy, an understanding of child development, active listening, and validation into your interactions with your children, you're doing more than just managing their behaviors. You're nurturing the development of their emotional intelligence. This contributes to a home environment where emotions are respected and expressed in healthy ways, laying the foundation for a lifetime of emotional resilience.

7.2 AGE-APPROPRIATE ANGER: ADJUSTING YOUR APPROACH

Navigating the intricacies of a child's anger requires a map that adapts to their growth, acknowledging that a toddler's tornado of fury is not the same as a teenager's tempest of rage. This segment explores the nuanced expressions of anger across different ages and stages, offering tailored ideas and strategies for managing these emotions and fostering constructive communication. From the ear-splitting screech of a discontented tot to the slamming doors of a temperamental teen, understanding and appropriately addressing our children's anger leads the way to emotional health and perseverance.

Understanding Anger at Different Developmental Stages

Children's capacity to understand, express, and manage their anger evolves dramatically from infancy through their teenage years. Recognizing these developmental milestones is crucial for responding in ways that nurture emotional growth.

- **Infants and toddlers**: At this stage, a baby or toddler's anger often emerges as a primal response to unfulfilled needs or overwhelming stimulation. Since their verbal communication skills are still budding, these little ones rely on crying and tantrums to express their wants, needs, or distress.
- **Preschoolers**: As children enter preschool age, their world gets bigger. More interactions bring more opportunities for frustration. They become more independent and stubborn, which can lead to massive power struggles. The "terrible twos" may become the "terrible threes."
- **School-age children**: Children's language skills tend to improve as they reach this stage, but they still might have trouble handling complex emotions. Figuring out social dynamics and how to get along with others can present new sources of frustration and anger.
- **Teenagers**: Adolescence brings a surge of hormonal changes that can intensify their emotions. Teens are

forming their identities, seeking autonomy, and often challenging authority figures, which can lead to conflicts.

Tailored Anger Management Strategies

Responding effectively to a child's anger involves strategies that align with their developmental level.

For Infants and Toddlers:

- **Comfort and calmness are key.** To help them settle down, hold them tenderly, talk to them soothingly, and remove them from overwhelming situations.
- **Distraction can be a powerful tool.** Redirecting their attention to a different activity or interesting object can diffuse frustration.

For Preschoolers:

- **Encourage the use of words to express their feelings.** Phrases like "Use your words to tell me what's wrong" can help them articulate their emotions.
- **Establish clear, consistent routines and boundaries.** Knowing what to expect reduces instances of frustration.

For School-Age Children:

- **Teach problem-solving skills.** When anger arises from a particular issue, encourage them to take the proper steps to find a solution. This bolsters their ability to manage their emotions constructively.
- **Promote empathy** by discussing how their actions affect

others, which helps broaden their understanding of emotions beyond their own.

For Teenagers:

- **Listen attentively without instant judgment or solutions.** Teens value being heard and understood without immediate parental intervention.
- **Encourage self-reflection.** Prompt your teen to consider the root cause of their anger and find healthy outlets for expressing it.

Communication Techniques for Each Age

Effective communication about anger varies with each developmental stage. It should be adapted accordingly to the child's growing cognitive and emotional capacities.

For Infants and Toddlers:

- **Use simple, calming words and phrases.** Even if they don't fully understand, the tone of your voice can provide great comfort.
- **Model calm behavior.** Children of this age are sponges and learn from watching how adults handle their own emotions.

For Preschoolers:

- **Visual aids**, like emotion charts, make it easier to identify and express their feelings.
- **Offer choices within limits.** Presenting them with

choices gives them a sense of control and reduces frustration.

For School-Age Children:

- **Engage in role-playing scenarios** that allow them to practice expressing anger and frustration in healthy, acceptable ways.
- **Establish a 'cool-down' spot** in your home or an activity in which they can calm down when their emotions run rampant.

For Teenagers:

- **Initiate open-ended conversations** that invite them to share their thoughts and feelings.
- **Respect their need for privacy** and space, offering your support when they're ready to talk.

Case Studies

The following real-life examples illustrate how age-appropriate strategies can be applied to help manage children's anger effectively.

- **Case Study: Everett, Age 4**- Everett's frustration with sharing his toys led to frequent outbursts. To help him control his emotions, his parents started using timeouts not as punishment but as an opportunity for Everett to calm down. They also introduced a visual "feelings chart" that displayed a colorful range of emotions, each associated with a corresponding facial expression. When Everett felt overwhelmed or upset, he could point to the picture that best represented his feelings. Everett learned to identify and express his emotions, gradually reducing the intensity of his outbursts. His parents praised his efforts to articulate his feelings and share his toys, noticing a significant decrease in tantrums.

- **Case Study: Charlotte, Age 12-** Charlotte, a fiery preteen, repeatedly clashed with her parents over chores, leading to over-the-top shouting matches that left everyone on edge. To resolve this problem, Charlotte helped her parents create a chore chart that included special rewards for completing tasks. They also designated a "cool-down" corner in her room, which included calming activities, like crafting kits and drawing supplies. This approach helped Charlotte express her anger in a positive way. It also helped to alleviate tension and improved the overall dynamic of the family.

- **Case Study: Hunter, Age 16-** Hunter's anger often manifested through silence and withdrawal. His parents learned to give him space, initiating conversations with open-ended questions when he seemed more approachable. They encouraged Hunter to engage in physical activities, like jogging or playing basketball, as an outlet for his frustration. Over time, Hunter became more open and started sharing his feelings without being prompted.

These examples showcase the importance of adjusting our approach to managing anger and communication with our children as they grow. By meeting them at their developmental stage with understanding and age-appropriate strategies, we not only address the immediate challenges of anger but also guide our children toward a future where they can navigate their emotions with confidence and wisdom.

7.3 SPECIAL CONSIDERATIONS FOR NEURODIVERSE CHILDREN

Navigating the emotional landscape of neurodiverse children requires a distinctive set of maps that account for the diverse ways these children perceive, interact with, and respond to the world around them. The term "neurodiversity" encompasses a variety of neurological conditions, including ADHD, autism spectrum disorder, and others. By understanding and embracing the differences in brain function and behavioral characteristics of neurodiverse individuals, we can truly appreciate the natural variability among all humans.

Understanding Neurodiversity

Children who are neurodiverse often experience and process emotions differently than their neurotypical peers. These distinctions can manifest in several ways, such as heightened sensitivity to sensory inputs, difficulty in verbally expressing their feelings, or struggles in understanding social cues. Recognizing these differences is the first step toward effectively supporting your child's emotional well-being. Providing a safe and supportive environment for your child can go a long way in helping them thrive.

- **For a child with ADHD**, the world may feel like a never-ending stream of distractions, making it incredibly difficult to focus on one thing at a time.
- **A child on the autism spectrum** might find it challenging to interpret facial expressions or tone of voice, which can complicate social interactions and emotional connections.

Strategies for Children with ADHD, Autism, etc.

Modifying your approach to meet the specific needs of your neurodiverse child can make a significant difference in helping them manage their emotions and behaviors.

For children with ADHD:

- **Using visual aids and sticking to schedules** provides structure and predictability, reducing frustration and anxiety.
- **Breaking tasks into smaller, more straightforward steps** and offering frequent, positive feedback keeps them motivated and focused on what they are doing.

For children on the autism spectrum:

- **Create a quiet, personal space** where they can retreat and self-regulate when sensory inputs or emotions overwhelm them.
- **Use clear, concise language and visual aids** to communicate expectations and routines to minimize misunderstandings and stress.

Collaboration with Professionals

Building a support network that includes educational and health-care professionals is critical for understanding and addressing the emotional needs of neurodiverse children. These experts can offer valuable insights into your child's specific challenges and strengths, suggest effective strategies tailored to their needs, and provide support and resources for the entire family.

- **Regular meetings with teachers** and special education professionals can ensure your child's learning environment is supportive and accommodates their needs.
- **Neurodiversity-trained therapists** can help your child develop healthy coping strategies, social skills, and emotional regulation methods.

Creating a Supportive Environment

The home environment plays a pivotal role in supporting the emotional well-being of our neurodiverse children. A space that anticipates and responds to their needs can help them feel secure, understood, and cherished.

- **Consistency and predictability**: Maintain consistent routines and set clear rules to create a sense of stability and predictability. This can be especially comforting for children who are distressed by change and uncertainty.
- **Sensory considerations**: Be mindful of sensory sensitivities. Simple adjustments, such as reducing background noise and using softer lighting, can make a huge difference in your child's comfort level and ability to regulate their emotions.
- **Opportunities for choice and control**: Offer your child choices whenever possible, from selecting what they want to wear to deciding what to eat for lunch. This sense of control can boost their self-esteem and reduce feelings of helplessness or frustration.
- **Emotion regulation tools**: Equip your home with resources to help your child express and manage their emotions. These might include fidget toys, stress balls, weighted blankets, art supplies for creative expression, or a

designated calming corner with comfortable cushions and favorite soothing objects.

When it comes to navigating the emotional landscape of neurodiverse children, patience, understanding, and creativity are your best allies. By embracing neurodiversity, using tailored strategies, collaborating with professionals, and maintaining a supportive home environment, you can guide your child through the intricacies of their emotions and behaviors, helping them build confidence, resilience, and a strong sense of self-worth.

7.4 EMOTIONAL INTELLIGENCE: TEACHING YOUR CHILD TO UNDERSTAND AND MANAGE EMOTIONS

Emotional intelligence (also known as emotional quotient or EQ) is the ability to recognize, understand, and manage our own emotions, as well as to recognize, understand, and influence the emotions of others. In children, developing emotional intelligence is imperative for working through social complexities, building relationships, and achieving personal and academic goals. EQ is the cornerstone of empathy, resilience, and communication, all of which are essential skills for success and well-being.

Parents play a pivotal role in nurturing emotional intelligence in their children, primarily through the examples they set. As we know, kids are very observant creatures who tend to imitate the emotional behaviors they see at home. When you express your emotions in a healthy, constructive way, you provide a live-action demonstration of EQ. For instance, by openly discussing your feelings of anxiety about an upcoming work presentation or your disappointment about missing a friend's wedding and how you plan to address them, you're showing your kids that it's normal to feel upset, but it's important to work through those emotions in a positive way.

Teaching your children about emotional intelligence doesn't have to be a formal lesson; you can easily incorporate it into your daily interactions and routines. Here are some tools and activities that can help:

- **Emotion labeling**: Encourage your children to name their feelings. From a young age, you can help them expand their emotional vocabulary beyond "happy" or "sad" to more nuanced terms like "frustrated," "anxious," or "excited." This helps them identify their own emotions and to recognize and empathize with the feelings of others.
- **Problem-solving together**: When conflicts or challenges arise, work together to identify the emotions at play and formulate solutions. This teaches children that emotions are cues, not obstacles, which helps them understand their feelings and think carefully about how to address them.
- **Role-playing games**: Use role-play to explore different scenarios and emotions. It's a fun way to practice empathy and see things from another person's point of view, which are vital components of EQ.
- **Feelings journal**: For older children, keeping a journal about their feelings can provide insight into their emotional patterns and triggers. It's a safe space for self-reflection and understanding the connection between their thoughts, feelings, and deeds.

The benefits of cultivating high emotional intelligence in our children are extensive. Not only does it lay the groundwork for building richer and more empathetic relationships, but it also correlates with educational achievements. Children with high EQ are better prepared to handle stress, navigate social situations, and make informed decisions— qualities that contribute to success both inside and outside the classroom.

Additionally, as our children grow and mature, their emotional intelligence becomes a key factor in their overall well-being. It helps them build resilience, allowing them to bounce back from adversities with a positive attitude and a healthy perspective. It also enhances their self-awareness, self-regulation, and integrity, guiding them to make choices that align with their moral values and aspirations.

By nurturing our children's emotional intelligence, we're preparing them with the tools they need to thrive in this uncertain world. We're helping them build a foundation of compassion and empathy that will serve them well throughout their lives, enriching their relationships and enabling them to face challenges with confidence and grace.

Let's never underestimate the profound impact our example and guidance have on our children's ability to traverse their emotional landscapes. By prioritizing EQ in our parenting, we're not just addressing immediate behaviors or conflicts; we're investing in our children's long-term stability, happiness, and success. With every conversation, every experience we share, and every moment of understanding, we're helping our children grow into compassionate, mindful adults who are ready to take on the world and make it a better place.

As we move on, let's keep these lessons with us, remembering the power of empathy, the importance of emotional vocabulary, and the value of demonstrating emotional intelligence in our everyday lives. Through our words and deeds, we can guide our children toward a brighter future marked by emotional wisdom and intense, meaningful connections.

8

DISCIPLINE WITH A HEART: SETTING LOVING BOUNDARIES

Imagine you're a sculptor, and your project is the growing, changing, and utterly unique personality of your child. Just as a sculptor uses special tools to gently but firmly shape their creation, setting boundaries is one of the tools parents use to help shape their children's understanding of the world, themselves, and how they fit into the grand scheme of life. It's a delicate balance that requires a blend of firmness, love, and the occasional step back to admire the beauty of the emerging masterpiece.

8.1 CREATING SAFE LIMITS: THE ROLE OF BOUNDARIES IN PARENTING

Importance of Clear Boundaries

Boundaries are like the frame around a painting; they don't constrain the art, they give it form, structure, and context. When children understand their limits, they feel safer and more secure. They know what's expected of them and what they can expect from others, which in turn helps them to explore, learn, and grow with confidence. It's a common misconception that boundaries stifle creativity or independence. On the contrary, they create a safe space where both can flourish.

How to Set Boundaries

Setting boundaries is less about laying down the law and more about guiding and teaching. It's a process, and like any good process, it has a few steps to follow:

- **Start with the why**: Before setting a boundary, know why it is necessary. Is it for safety or to teach respect? Understanding the 'why' helps you explain it to your child, making it more than just a rule—it becomes a lesson.
- **Be clear and specific**: Instead of using vague statements such as "Be good," try "Please use inside voices when we're in the library." This tells your child exactly what's expected.
- **Consistency is key**: A boundary only works if it's consistently applied. If bedtime is at 8 PM, then that's the rule, whether it's Monday or Friday. Consistency helps children internalize boundaries much more quickly.
- **Adjust as needed**: As your children grow, their boundaries will need to grow with them. Review boundaries regularly to ensure they're still relevant and modify them as necessary.

Involving Kids in Boundary-Setting

Involvement breeds commitment. When children participate in setting their boundaries, they're more likely to understand and respect them. It also teaches them valuable skills in negotiation and compromise. Here's how:

- **Age-appropriate choices**: Give your child choices within the boundaries you're setting. For example, "Would you like to do your homework before dinner or after?"
- **Discuss consequences**: Talk about the natural consequences of not respecting boundaries. This helps children understand the 'why' behind the rule.
- **Encourage input**: For older children, ask for their input on what boundaries should be set. You might be surprised at how reasonable they can be.

Maintaining Boundaries without Anger

When boundaries are pushed (as they certainly will be), it's not a sign of failure but a normal part of the learning process. Here's how to maintain them without resorting to anger and losing your cool:

- **Stay calm**: When a boundary is tested, take a deep breath before reacting. This helps you handle the situation calmly and firmly.
- **Use reminders**: Sometimes, all it takes is a gentle reminder. Simply saying, "Remember, we agreed on no snacks before dinner," can do the trick.
- **Positive reinforcement**: Whenever your child respects a boundary, acknowledge it. Positive reinforcement is very effective in encouraging good behavior.
- **Choose your battles**: Not every tested boundary requires a confrontation. Sometimes, letting the small things slide makes it easier to enforce the big stuff when it really matters.

At the end of the day, setting boundaries with patience and love is about teaching your children how to navigate their everyday lives safely and respectfully. It's an essential part of parenting and helps your children develop into well-rounded, dependable humans. By setting clear and consistent boundaries, involving your kids in the process, and maintaining the boundaries without losing your temper, you're not just disciplining them—you're teaching, guiding, and loving them every step of the way. So, go ahead and set those boundaries. As long as you set them with your children's best interests at heart, it's the best way to raise happy, healthy, obedient youngsters.

8.2 CONSEQUENCES VS. PUNISHMENT: A NEW PERSPECTIVE

When it comes to discipline, parents are often presented with a dichotomy: consequences versus punishment. It's a fine line, but understanding and applying the distinction when disciplining our children can significantly affect how they learn from their experiences.

Redefining Consequences

The concept of consequences is often lumped together with punishment, but they are fundamentally different. Consequences are the natural or logical outcomes of actions. They are not designed to inflict suffering but to teach important lessons. For example, if a child forgets their jacket on a cold, windy day, feeling chilly and uncomfortable is a natural consequence, inherently teaching them the importance of being prepared. On the other hand, punishment, such as taking away a favorite toy or privilege because the jacket was forgotten, will only lead to resentment and confusion without providing any real lesson on preparedness. The educational value of consequences lies in their ability to help children understand the connection between actions and outcomes, giving them a sense of responsibility and foresight.

Implementing Logical Consequences

The effectiveness of logical consequences depends on their direct relation and timely connection to the child's misbehavior. Instead of viewing them as punishment, it's important to see them as valuable learning opportunities. Here are some examples:

- **Not putting toys away**: Instead of a timeout, a logical consequence could be spending time organizing the playroom. This directly ties the outcome to the action, emphasizing responsibility.
- **Forgetting homework**: Rather than grounding, a more suitable consequence might be having them use their free time to catch up on missed assignments, which teaches time management and accountability.
- **Mistreating others**: Instead of a timeout or grounding, ask them to apologize or make amends, such as writing a letter of apology or doing something kind for the person they hurt. This teaches empathy and accountability.

These methods encourage children to reflect on their actions and understand the importance of making better choices in the future.

The Problem with Punitive Punishment

Punitive punishment can create a rift in the parent-child relationship, often leaving children feeling wronged and resentful. It focuses on the child's failures rather than the learning opportunity, potentially stunting their emotional growth. Punishments like these can instill fear instead of understanding, leading to behavioral changes out of anxiety rather than a genuine comprehension of right and wrong. The emotional toll of punitive punishment can also erode trust, making children less likely to confide in their parents about their problems or mistakes in fear of harsh judgment or penalties.

Transitioning to a Consequence-based Approach

Switching from a punishment-based system to one rooted in logical consequences requires patience and consistency, but the rewards are abundant. Here's how to make the transition:

- **Open dialogue**: Start with a family discussion about the new approach to discipline. Explain the difference between punitive punishment and logical consequences, emphasizing the focus on learning and growth.
- **Involve children in the process**: When setting up consequences for potential misbehaviors, involve your children. This can help them understand the reasoning behind the rules and the fairness of the consequences, making them more likely to accept and learn from them.
- **Be consistent**: Apply consequences consistently. If a certain action always leads to the same consequence, children will quickly learn the connection between their choices and the outcomes.
- **Focus on the future**: After a consequence has been applied, talk with your child about what they've learned and how they can make better choices going forward. This reinforces the lesson and helps them to always remember it.

Shifting your focus from punitive punishment to logical consequences not only helps with the immediate resolution of your children's misbehaviors but also plays a vital role in teaching them about cause and effect, taking responsibility for their actions, and making amends. It lays the basis for your children to develop into conscientious, considerate individuals who understand the impact of their actions. This approach contributes to a healthier parent-child dynamic. It prepares children with the wisdom, insight, and empathy they need to conquer life's inevitable challenges both inside and outside the home.

8.3 CONSISTENCY IS KEY: THE IMPORTANCE OF FOLLOWING THROUGH

When guiding our children toward understanding right from wrong and helping them develop self-discipline, the steadiness of our approach is crucial. Imagine planting a garden where you water the seeds sporadically, sometimes flooding them and at other times leaving them parched for days. The results would be unpredictable at best. Likewise, when we fluctuate in our disciplinary methods, we risk sending mixed signals to our children, making it harder for them to understand the boundaries we've set and the behaviors we expect from them.

The Role of Consistency in Discipline

Consistency in discipline acts as the steady rain that nurtures the garden of our children's understanding and behavior. It solidifies our expectations, making it clear to them what is acceptable and what is not. This clarity provides a sense of security and trust. Children thrive when they know the parameters in which they are allowed to explore and which lines they should not cross. This reliability helps children internalize discipline and regulate their own behavior over time.

Challenges to Consistency

Despite our best intentions, maintaining a consistent disciplinary approach can be daunting. Life throws those darned curveballs our way, whether it's an unexpected bill, an illness, or just the relentless momentum of our daily routines. These situations can make it tempting to let things slide or react based on our stress levels rather than sticking to our carefully established guidelines.

- **Fatigue and stress**: At the end of a long, exhausting day, it's easier to give in and say "yes" just to avoid conflict, even when it goes against our previously set rules.
- **Differing parenting styles**: When co-parents use different methods of discipline, it can be confusing for children to understand what's expected of them.
- **Lack of immediate results**: Sometimes, the impact of consistent discipline isn't immediately visible, leading to frustration and potentially slacking off our efforts.

Strategies for Consistent Discipline

Overcoming these challenges is not impossible. A few proactive strategies can help you stay on course, even when the going gets rough.

- **Plan ahead**: Discuss and agree on discipline strategies ahead of time. Having a clear plan can help prevent impulsive, emotion-driven decisions.
- **Unified front**: If you're co-parenting, be sure you are both on the same page regarding discipline. Presenting a united front prevents children from playing one parent against the other.

- **Simple rules**: Keep rules straightforward and simple. It's easier to be consistent with a few clear rules rather than a long list of complicated ones.
- **Self-care**: Taking care of your physical and emotional well-being makes it easier to maintain consistency. You're less likely to react out of stress or fatigue when you're well-rested and centered.
- **Routine checks**: Review your discipline strategies regularly to ensure they are still relevant and practical. Adjustments may be necessary as your child grows and matures.

The Impact of Inconsistency

Inconsistency can muddy the waters of discipline. When children receive mixed messages about what's expected of them, it can lead to confusion and insecurity. They may test boundaries more frequently, trying to figure out what their limits truly are. This can result in more behavioral issues, not fewer. Inconsistency can also weaken the parent-child bond, as children may feel they cannot rely on their parents to be steady and fair.

In this ever-changing world, providing our children with consistency in our expectations and responses creates a safe harbor for them. It's a place where they can anchor their understanding of right and wrong and learn to manage their behavior in a way that's respectful to themselves and others. While achieving this level of consistency demands effort and mindfulness, the rewards of seeing our children evolve into responsible, self-disciplined individuals are well worth it.

8.4 THE TEACHABLE MOMENT: TURNING MISTAKES INTO LEARNING OPPORTUNITIES

Life, with all its intricacies, offers us a medley of moments that, although they might seem trivial or challenging at first, hold within them the seeds for growth and learning. Whether it's the spilled milk, the crayon marks on the wall, or the shattered vase, each occurrence is fertile ground for what I like to call "teachable moments." With care and thoughtful consideration, we can turn these simple missteps into valuable lessons for our children, guiding them toward a path of self-improvement and empathy.

Identifying Teachable Moments

Turning mistakes into learning opportunities depends on our ability to recognize these moments for what they truly are: golden chances for growth. It starts with observing not just our children's actions but peeling back the layers to understand the context. Was the milk spilled by accident, because of absent-mindedness, or out of plain curiosity? Each scenario presents a unique lesson waiting to be uncovered. The key here is to have patience and an open mind. This allows us to see past the inconvenience of the moment and into the potential it holds for teaching critical life skills such as responsibility, mindfulness, or the value of curiosity.

Guiding Children Through Reflection

Reflection is the mirror through which we can view our actions, understand their consequences, and visualize alternative routes. Encouraging our children to look into this mirror involves more than just asking them why they did whatever they did. It's about guiding them to think about how their actions affected themselves and others, what emotions led to those actions, and how they might handle a similar situation differently in the future. Asking them open-ended questions prompts deeper thinking, while maintaining a non-judgmental tone helps them feel safe in fully exploring their thoughts and emotions.

Encouraging Problem-Solving

Equipping our children with the tools to solve problems on their own fosters independence. It also instills confidence in their ability to overcome life's many hurdles. When a child makes a mistake, instead of rushing to rectify it ourselves, we can ask, "What do you think is the best way to fix this?" Questions like these encourage our kids to use their critical thinking and creativity to find solutions. It's also beneficial to walk through potential solutions together, weighing the pros and cons, which teaches decision-making skills and the importance of considering different outcomes.

Celebrating Growth

Every step forward, no matter how small, is a victory in the journey of learning and growth. Recognizing and celebrating each milestone reinforces positive behavior and motivates further improvement. Did your child take responsibility for their mistake without being prompted? Did they come up with a thoughtful solution to a problem they caused? Acknowledging these achievements with praise or some kind of reward works wonders for their self-esteem and encourages them to keep applying what they've learned. It's a cycle of positive reinforcement, where each success builds upon the last, creating an unstoppable momentum of growth and learning.

Incorporating these principles into our parenting allows us to view our children's mistakes not as shortcomings but as stepping stones that lead us to greater insight and understanding. This perspective enables us to see beyond the moment of our children's misconduct and recognize the vast possibilities each mistake offers for teaching, learning, and personal development. This approach not only helps us find healthy resolutions for wayward behavior, but it also plays an essential role in shaping our children into kind, responsible, and resilient adults who do well in this world. Let's embrace this mindset, cherishing life's teachable moments and using them to guide our children toward reaching their fullest potential.

9

CRAFTING A FAMILY CULTURE OF OPENNESS

Picture a warm, inviting scene where everyone in the family, from the littlest one with a sticky, chocolate-stained face to the eldest with a few years of wisdom under their belt, gathers around the cozy living room. Each person openly and enthusiastically shares their thoughts, concerns, and laughter. This isn't just a dreamy fantasy of family life or something you only see on The Brady Bunch; it's absolutely achievable! All it takes is something as simple yet profound as a family meeting.

9.1 THE FAMILY MEETING: SETTING THE STAGE FOR OPEN COMMUNICATION

Facilitating Open Dialogue

Creating a safe space for open conversation means setting up a zone in your home that's entirely free of judgment, criticism, and distractions. Each family member's voice is equally valued, no matter how loud, high-pitched, or soft it may be. It's basically turning your living room into a miniature democracy where everyone gets a vote. Here's how to achieve this:

- **Start by explaining the purpose of the meeting.** It's not just about airing grievances; it's also about sharing wins, worries, wonders, and discussing family matters.
- **Use a "talking stick"** or any object that can be held by the speaker. This adds a touch of formality and clearly marks whose turn it is to speak, teaching kids patience and respect for others while waiting for their turn to share.

Scheduling Regular Meetings

Consistency is paramount. Picking a regular time, such as every Sunday evening or the first Friday of every month, helps to make these meetings a natural part of your family's rhythm. Why it works:

- **It gives everyone something to look forward to** and plan their schedules around.
- **Regularity builds trust.** When kids know they'll have a chance to speak up and be heard at these meetings, they might be more inclined to save their concerns for the meeting when everyone is present.

Using Inclusive Language

The words we choose can build bridges or create walls. Using "we" statements promotes a sense of teamwork and collective accountability. For example:

- Instead of "You need to clean your room," it might be better to say, "We all have a responsibility to keep our home neat and tidy. How can we help each other with this?" This approach not only softens demands but also emphasizes the family as a unit, working together towards common goals.

Encouraging Participation from All Family Members

Every family member has unique insights and opinions, making their contributions invaluable. Here's how to ensure each person gets a fair chance to share what's on their mind:

- **For little ones who may not be as verbal**, encourage them to draw a picture or show something that represents their thoughts or feelings.
- **Set a rule that no one can interrupt** when someone is speaking. This teaches respect and the importance of listening attentively.

A family meeting agenda template could be a helpful visual aid for those who can read. These templates have sections for compliments, concerns, and creative solutions. (Look for one online that you can print to ensure a balanced and productive meeting.)

Why does all of this matter? Because in the hustle and bustle of daily life, with school, work, and endless activities pulling us in different directions, having a dedicated time and space for genuine family connection ensures that no one feels left behind or unheard. It's about creating a family culture where openness, empathy, and understanding prosper. This sets the stage for a peaceful home environment and nurtures well-rounded individuals who will carry these values into the world.

Through these meetings, you're not just discussing trivial issues like who took the last cookie; you're also catching up and finding out what can be done to better support one another through trials and tribulations. This special time reinforces the bonds that make your family unique and resilient. It's in these gatherings around the dinner table or in the living room where the magic of understanding and connection happens, problems find solutions, and the family's hearts beat with unity, strength, and love.

9.2 RULES OF ENGAGEMENT: ESTABLISHING FAMILY GROUND RULES FOR EXPRESSING ANGER

When tempers flare, it's like a hurricane brewing on the horizon. Without some sort of plan, that storm can sweep throughout the home, leaving confusion and hurt feelings in its wake. But imagine having a set of guidelines, a family pact, designed to steer us through these tempestuous times with compassion and understanding. This is where the real work of building a nurturing family environment begins.

Creating Constructive Rules

A fundamental step in managing anger constructively within your household is to lay down some ground rules. Think of these rules as an infrastructure for expressing emotions in a healthy and respectful way. The goal isn't to suppress anger—after all, it's a natural human emotion—but to learn to express it in ways that don't cause harm or worsen the situation.

- **Sit down as a family and discuss what behaviors are off-limits.** Yelling, name-calling, cursing, or door-slamming might be a few of the actions you agree to avoid.
- **Decide on what actions should be encouraged** when someone feels angry. Perhaps taking a few deep breaths,

asking for a time-out, or using "I feel" statements to express upset feelings constructively.

The Importance of Consistency

For these rules to be effective, they must be applied consistently. This means that every family member, including parents, must adhere to the agreed-upon guidelines. Consistency is the backbone of trust within the family; it assures each person that their home is a stable and safe space where their emotions can be predictably and calmly managed.

- **Create a visual reminder** of these rules, such as a poster on the living room wall or a magnet on the refrigerator as a constant hint to follow them.
- **When rules are broken**, address the offense gently but firmly, reminding those involved of the agreed-upon guidelines and discussing ways to handle their emotions better next time.

Involving Everyone in Rule-Making

Involvement in creating these rules ensures everyone feels invested in them. It's a collaborative effort that acknowledges each person's feelings and opinions are valid and worthy of recognition. This collective approach strengthens the family's commitment to these guidelines. It empowers each member, giving them a sense of ownership over their emotional well-being and their role in maintaining a harmonious home.

- **Hold a family meeting** dedicated to formulating these rules. Give everyone, young and old, a chance to express their opinions on what should be included.

- **For younger children who might not be able to verbalize** their thoughts as clearly, have them draw or act out behaviors they think are okay and not okay when someone is mad.

Examples of Effective Ground Rules

Ground rules can vary from one family to another. Several commonly effective guidelines have helped maintain peace and understanding in many households across the globe. Here are a few:

- **"We talk, we don't yell"**: This rule emphasizes the importance of using a calm, normal-speaking voice, even when discussing something that makes us angry or upset.
- **"We take turns speaking"**: This ensures that everyone has a chance to express their feelings without being interrupted, maintaining an air of respect and patience.
- **"We take a time-out when needed"**: Recognizing when we're too upset to continue a constructive conversation and taking a break to cool down can prevent conflicts from escalating.
- **"We use 'I feel' statements"**: Encouraging expressions such as "I feel upset when..." instead of accusatory statements promotes understanding and empathy.

Implementing these rules might seem daunting at first, but over time, they become second nature, ingrained into your family's daily life. They act as beacons, guiding each person through the frequently dense fog of emotions, ensuring that even when anger arises, it will be handled with care, respect, and love. Through these guidelines, parents and children learn not just to manage their anger but also to understand and appreciate each other's emotional attributes, forging deeper connections and a richer, more loving bond that lasts a lifetime.

9.3 SUPPORT SYSTEMS: BUILDING A NETWORK OF CARE FOR EACH FAMILY MEMBER

I like to think of family life as an exquisite painting, where each brush stroke - every laugh, disagreement, and comforting embrace contributes to the beauty and warmth of the whole. Each family member enhances this breathtaking creation with their own vividly unique hues of radiant colors, resulting in a stunning work of art.

Recognizing and nurturing the individual needs of each person in the family cultivates a sense of harmony that brings everyone together as a united front, just like the colors in a painting work in unison to create a symphony of magic on canvas. Here, we'll discuss how we can identify and meet these needs, expand our network of care beyond the immediate family, and weave empathy into every interaction, creating a support system that uplifts and sustains each member.

Identifying Support Needs

Every family member has specific needs for support, from the toddler trying to figure out how to use their words to the teenager on the brink of adulthood and the parents constantly juggling multiple roles in between. Identifying these needs is the first step in fortifying the family network.

- **Take time for individual check-ins**: This could be during a quiet chat over a cup of hot chocolate or a casual walk around the neighborhood. The goal is to create a safe space where each person feels comfortable opening up about their needs, whether they're emotional, such as needing to feel heard, or practical, like needing help with schoolwork.

- **Pay attention to non-verbal signals**: Children sometimes have trouble articulating their needs for support. Changes in behavior or mood can be telltale signs that they need a helping hand or a listening ear.
- **Celebrate individuality within the family**: Acknowledge and support each person's interests and talents. This not only bolsters self-esteem but also clarifies where they might need support to pursue their passions.

External Support Networks

While your immediate family is an incredible source of support, sometimes we can all use extra help in one form or another. Expanding your network to include friends, extended family, and community resources enriches the support available, offering diverse perspectives and resources. These options are helpful when you need additional assistance.

- **Friends and extended family** can be your saving grace in times of need, providing emotional support as well as physical help, such as babysitting or tutoring.
- **Community resources**, from after-school programs to family counseling services, offer specialized support that can meet your specific needs. This can help alleviate pressure for you and your family and create a sense of belonging and connection to your community.
- **Consider looking into online communities** and forums for support in areas where distance might be a problem. These platforms can offer invaluable advice and insight.

Connecting with other parents facing the same issues can help you not feel so alone.

Creating a Family Support Plan

A family support plan helps ensure each family member's needs are met. It involves pooling resources and scheduling regular check-ins. This plan, co-created with input from parents and children, can act as your roadmap for effectively managing, supporting, and meeting everyone's needs in times of crisis or whenever necessary.

- **Start with a family meeting** to discuss and document each person's needs and how they can be met, both within and outside the family.
- **Assign responsibilities** but be flexible. Life is unpredictable, and the plan should accommodate changes and shifts in needs and availability.
- **Set up a family calendar.** Include regular check-ins, appointments for professional support services, and family activities everyone enjoys for relaxation and reconnection.
- **Keep a resource list** easily accessible to all family members. Include phone numbers for trusted friends and extended family, as well as contact information for external support sources, such as family therapists and community centers.

The Role of Empathy in Support

At the core of any robust family support system, you'll find empathy. It's not just a concept but the thread that binds the entire network, ensuring that each act of support is infused with love, understanding, and compassion.

- **Practice active listening.** When a family member expresses their needs, listen with the intent to understand them, not to respond. This validates their feelings and shows them that their needs matter.
- **Create an environment where asking for help** is encouraged and not seen as a weakness. This starts with parents modeling vulnerability, showing that it's okay to not have all the answers and to lean on others for support.
- **Empathize with failures and celebrate successes equally.** Support isn't just for the tough times; it's also about being there to cheer on and uplift each other in moments of victory.

By creating a support system that extends from within the walls of our home into the community around us and back, we are building a wholesome network of care that upholds each family member. This network, grounded in empathy and enriched by diverse sources of support, ensures that each person is seen, heard, and taken care of. Through this, our family unit grows stronger, more resilient, and tightly bonded, ready to face the joys and sorrows that lie ahead together.

9.4 CELEBRATING SUCCESS: RECOGNIZING AND REWARDING EFFORTS TO MANAGE ANGER

In the same way that sunlight nurtures seeds into a lush green garden, recognizing and celebrating each family member's efforts to manage their anger can nurture growth and positive change. Shining a light on even the smallest steps forward can make the journey toward better anger management feel rewarding and achievable for everyone involved.

Acknowledging Progress

It's important to point out and commend your child when you see that they're making an effort to control their anger, no matter how insignificant it may seem. This could be as simple as saying, "I noticed you took a deep breath when you were getting upset earlier. You did a great job staying calm." These moments of recognition affirm that your child's efforts to change are valued and seen, reinforcing their desire to continue improving.

- **Make it a point during family meetings to spotlight these efforts.** This shows appreciation and demonstrates to everyone that progress is being made, which can be incredibly motivating.
- **Personal acknowledgments** catered to each individual's efforts can make the recognition feel more genuine and impactful.

Setting up a Reward System

Implementing a system that rewards efforts and achievements in managing anger can further motivate and encourage children. This system doesn't need to be elaborate; it can be as simple as earning stickers for younger ones or earning points toward a family outing of their choice for older kids.

- **Decide as a family what rewards would be the most meaningful and attainable.** This ensures everyone is on board with the system and excited about the rewards.
- **Keep the system transparent and fair,** with clearly defined ways for each child to earn the rewards. This clarity helps everyone maintain trust in the process and keeps them motivated to participate.

Celebrating Small Wins

Every step in the right direction deserves recognition and praise. Celebrating these wins, regardless of their size, boosts everyone's enthusiasm and keeps the momentum going. It could be a special treat to celebrate a day without temper tantrums or choosing what's for dinner after a week of using positive communication.

- **Create traditions to celebrate these wins**, such as making a favorite dessert or reading an extra story at bedtime. These become cherished family traditions and something your children always look forward to.
- **Encourage everyone to share their wins**, no matter how small they might think they are. This builds a spirit of positivity and encouragement that inspires the entire family.

Sharing Success Stories

When one person shares their success story, it becomes a ray of hope for everyone else. Maybe a child managed to express their frustrations calmly instead of throwing a fit, or perhaps another found a new technique that helped them cool down quickly. Sharing these stories can:

- **Provide useful strategies and insights** others might not have considered, offering new ideas for managing anger.
- **Inspire and motivate** everyone by showing that change is indeed possible and that the efforts to manage anger in healthier ways are worth it.

The path to managing anger within a family is multifaceted. It requires patience, dedication, effort, and a lot of heart. Open communication, setting clear rules, building a network of support, and celebrating each victory along the way are all vital steps to success. These efforts not only help in managing anger but also in strengthening the unbreakable bonds of love and understanding that hold a family together.

Let's remember the lessons we've learned and the victories won. In these moments, the true essence of family is found—not in the absence of conflict but in the way we come together as a team to endure, understand, and grow from it.

10

SEEKING HELP: KNOWING WHEN AND HOW

So there you are, in the kitchen, preparing dinner for your hungry family. You've got all your ingredients lined up, the recipe is in front of you, and you're ready to go. But then, you try to preheat the oven and discover it isn't working. Your partner, who usually repairs things, is out of town. You try a few quick fixes, frantically look at the manual, and even ask a friend for advice over the phone. Regardless of your desperate measures, the oven remains cold and unresponsive. At this point (and possibly after a few colorful obscenities), you recognize it's time to call in a professional. This moment you realize that despite your best efforts, you need external help, is the same journey many families face when dealing with anger issues. It may be difficult to accept, but it's important to acknowledge when your usual tools and strategies aren't enough and understand that seeking professional help is okay and can be profoundly beneficial to you and your family.

10.1 UNDERSTANDING THE SIGNS: WHEN TO SEEK PROFESSIONAL HELP FOR YOURSELF AND YOUR FAMILY

Recognizing Red Flags

The first step in seeking help is to identify the signs that indicate it might be time to reach out for professional support. These signs can manifest in various ways within the family:

- **Persistent conflict that isn't resolved** through communication or by using the strategies outlined in previous chapters could signify underlying issues that may require professional intervention.
- **Physical aggression** or violence toward oneself or others is a clear sign that immediate help is needed. Addressing these behaviors early on is crucial for everyone's safety and well-being.
- **Signs of depression or anxiety**, such as prolonged sadness, withdrawal from activities, significant changes in sleeping or eating patterns, or expressions of hopelessness, should not be disregarded. Mental health issues impact not just the individual but the entire family as well.
- **High levels of stress** that are out of control and affect daily functioning can seriously erode a family's happiness and well-being. Chronic stress can lead to a host of mental and physical health problems and requires urgent professional intervention.

Recognizing these red flags early on can prevent further escalation and start you and your family on the journey toward healing and understanding.

Monitoring Changes in Behavior

Changes in behavior, especially those that are sudden or drastic, can indicate deeper issues. Keeping a close eye on how each family member is coping in their daily lives can help you catch potential problems early:

- **Withdrawal from family or social activities** and preferring to be alone may suggest a person is struggling.
- **Sudden declines in school performance** or a loss of interest in previously enjoyed activities can be signs of emotional distress in children and teenagers.
- **Increased irritability or mood swings** that seem out of character should not be dismissed. Emotional fluctuations are normal to a certain extent (especially in the teen years), but extreme changes can be a red flag.

The Impact of Stress on Mental Health

Stress, although it's a normal part of life, can profoundly affect our mental health when it becomes chronic. It's essential to understand the following:

- **Chronic stress can manifest in physical symptoms**, such as headaches, fatigue, and changes in appetite, and in emotional symptoms, such as irritability, anxiety, and depression.
- **It's important to manage stress** through healthy outlets and, when necessary, seek professional help to prevent it from undermining the family's quality of life.

Self-Assessment Tools

Self-assessment tools can be valuable for evaluating whether the challenges you're facing require professional intervention. These tools can offer insights into:

- **The severity of symptoms** being experienced by you or your family members.
- **The impact of these symptoms** on your daily life and ability to function.
- **Whether these challenges are beyond the scope** of your usual coping mechanisms or self-help strategies and require professional guidance.

These assessments are not diagnostic tools but can help you decide if it's time to seek professional support. Many reputable mental health organizations offer free, confidential online assessments, which can be a good starting point.

When you recognize that it might be time to seek help, it's crucial to remember that reaching out shows strength, not weakness. It demonstrates a commitment to your family's well-being and a willingness to take the steps necessary to ensure it. Your vigilance and determination to manage anger by seeking professional guidance can make all the difference in restoring peace and harmony in your home.

10.2 FINDING THE RIGHT HELP: RESOURCES FOR PARENTS

Seeking help to manage anger for yourself or within the family can feel like trying to solve a puzzle while the pieces keep changing shape. Knowing where to start or what kind of help will fit your family's unique needs can be confusing. Let's walk through this process, breaking it down into simple steps that make finding the right support less intimidating and more attainable.

Navigating Mental Health Services

The mental health system can seem like a labyrinth, especially when you're looking for specific support for anger management issues within a family context. Here are some pointers to guide your way:

- **Start with a general practitioner (GP)**: Your regular doctor can be an excellent first point of contact. They can offer initial advice, rule out any underlying medical conditions that may contribute to your anger issues, and refer you to specialist services if needed.
- **Mental health professionals**: Understanding the different roles of mental health professionals can help you decide who to call. Psychologists can provide therapy and strategies for managing anger, while psychiatrists are medical doctors who can prescribe medication if necessary.
- **Specialized services**: Look for professionals or services that specialize in family therapy or have specific experience in treating anger management. These experts can provide targeted strategies that address the root of the issues.

Evaluating Professionals

Once you've narrowed down a few potential therapists or counselors, how do you determine which one is the right fit for you? Here are some criteria and questions to take into account:

- **Qualifications and experience**: Check their qualifications and ensure they're registered with a reputable professional organization. Experience in working with families and dealing with anger management is of utmost importance.
- **Approach to therapy**: Therapists usually have different approaches, so finding one that aligns with your family's specific needs is essential. Ask about their methods and how they involve family members in the process.
- **Comfort level**: The right therapist should make you and your family feel comfortable and safe. It's okay to trust your gut feeling here.
- **Availability and accessibility**: Consider their availability to accommodate your family's schedule and if they offer virtual sessions, which can provide greater flexibility.

Questions to Ask Potential Providers:

- Can you share your experience with family therapy and anger management?
- How do you involve children/teens in the therapy process?
- What's your approach to handling conflicts that may arise during therapy sessions?

Insurance and Affordability

The cost of therapy can be a concern, but there are ways to make it more affordable:

- **Insurance coverage**: Check with your insurance provider to see what mental health services are covered under your policy. Some plans cover family therapy or offer a certain number of sessions with a psychologist or counselor.

- **Sliding scale fees**: Many therapists offer sliding scale fees based on income, making therapy more accessible to families with different financial situations.
- **Community mental health centers**: These centers often provide services at a reduced cost or even for free. Although there might be waiting lists, they can be a great resource for families in need.

Community and Online Resources

Sometimes, the support you need can be found closer to home or even online. Here are some resources you might want to explore:

- **Local support groups**: Many communities have support groups where families dealing with similar issues can share their experiences and offer advice. These groups can provide a sense of belonging and understanding. It's a great way to meet new people and make friends.
- **Online forums and support networks**: Online platforms can offer a wealth of information and support. Websites dedicated to family therapy, parenting, and mental health often host forums where you can ask questions and learn from others' experiences.
- **Educational workshops and seminars**: Keep an eye out for workshops or seminars on anger management or family dynamics. These can be great opportunities to learn new strategies and even meet professionals.

Finding the right help for you and your family doesn't have to be an overwhelming endeavor. With the proper information and a bit of guidance, you can easily navigate the mental health system, evaluate potential therapists, and access community and online resources that can support your family's journey toward managing anger in a healthy, constructive way. Remember, reaching out for help is a positive step towards achieving a happy home environment where your children can prosper.

10.3 THERAPY AS A FAMILY: WORKING TOGETHER TOWARDS SOLUTIONS

When the idea of therapy comes up in family discussions, it often brings a mix of feelings to the surface. Some might feel hopeful, thinking this could be the turning point towards happier times. Others might feel apprehensive, unsure of what to expect, and worried about revealing their innermost thoughts and feelings. Entering therapy as a family is a lot like deciding to renovate your home. It's like recognizing that even though the structure is solid, some rooms might need a fresh coat of paint, or maybe the layout should be reconsidered to better suit everyone's needs.

The Benefits of Family Therapy

Participating in family therapy offers numerous advantages that go beyond addressing individual concerns. It's about mending the lines of communication that may have frayed over time and ensuring that every voice within the household feels heard and validated. Here's what makes it stand out:

- **Strengthened bonds**: By engaging in therapy together, families often discover new depths and greater meaning in their relationships. It's a safe space where misunderstandings can be unraveled, and an appreciation for each other's feelings and perspectives can grow.
- **Improved communication**: Therapy provides tools to enhance how family members talk to and understand each

other. Learning to express emotions and needs productively can positively transform daily interactions.

- **Resolving deep-seated issues**: Sometimes, families get stuck in a rut because unresolved issues keep resurfacing. Therapy can help get to the bottom of these underlying problems, breaking the cycle of blame and resentment.
- **Developing coping strategies**: Life will always have its challenges. Therapy equips families with strategies and coping mechanisms to handle stressful situations and conflicts more effectively.

Setting Goals for Therapy

Walking into therapy without an objective in mind can feel like sailing across the ocean without a compass. Deciding ahead of time what your goals are helps to focus the sessions and gives everyone a clear sense of direction and purpose. Here's how to approach this:

- **Identify what you want to change**: Start by having an open family discussion about what isn't working and what everyone hopes to achieve through therapy. This could include wanting to feel closer as a family, learning how to get along without fighting, or how to support a family member going through a hard time.
- **Be realistic and specific**: Strive for realistic and attainable goals. Instead of a broad objective like "improve family happiness," focus on specific changes you'd like to see, such as "reduce the frequency of arguments" or "spend quality time together at least once a week."
- **Flexibility is key**: As you progress in therapy, your goals might evolve. Be sure to review them periodically and

adjust them as needed, so they continue to reflect everyone's needs.

Active Participation

For therapy to work its magic, the participation of every family member is crucial. It's like a team sport where the outcome of the game depends entirely on the effort put forth by each player. Here's how you can encourage active involvement:

- **Create a safe space**: Confirm that every family member feels safe openly sharing their thoughts and feelings without fear of judgment or repercussions. This might mean agreeing to the rules about how discussions are conducted, both within therapy and at home.
- **Value each contribution**: Emphasize the importance of each family member's input. When children feel that their ideas and opinions matter, they're more likely to fully engage in the process.
- **Commit to the work**: Therapy is not just limited to the sessions. The entire family must commit to working on the strategies and exercises suggested by the therapist and recognize that progress requires dedication and consistent effort.

Confidentiality and Trust

Trust is the cornerstone of effective therapy. Worrying about confidentiality, especially among family members, can make it hard to open up and share. Here's how you can navigate these concerns:

- **Understand the ground rules**: Therapists are bound by confidentiality agreements, meaning that anything shared in therapy stays in therapy. However, the dynamics might be slightly different in family therapy since whatever is discussed involves everyone present. For extra reassurance, have the therapist explain how confidentiality is handled in this context.
- **Building trust within the family**: Agreeing as a family to respect the confidentiality of whatever is shared in therapy sessions helps build trust. It's about ensuring that the therapy space is respected as a haven for honesty, without fear of repercussions outside of that space.
- **Open dialogue about concerns**: If there are any worries about privacy or trust, don't hesitate to bring them up in therapy. Addressing these issues openly can be a vital step in strengthening family relationships.

Entering family therapy is a courageous step toward healing and growth. It's a commitment to improving the lives of each individual and enriching the collective family spirit. In this sacred, shared space, every frustration, every tear, but also every laugh and triumph becomes another stitch that knits the family closer together. With open hearts and minds, a willingness to change, and faithful dedication to the process, families can work through their issues and emerge as a united front, ready to take on whatever comes their way.

10.4 BREAKING THE STIGMA: NORMALIZING THERAPY FOR MENTAL HEALTH

In the world of today, while there have been major breakthroughs in the studies of mental health, the stigma around seeking professional help continues to be a significant barrier for those who genuinely need it. Feelings of shame and embarrassment often prevent people who struggle with their mental health from pursuing treatment. It's time for a change, and it starts within our homes and communities. By actively challenging misconceptions and openly discussing mental health, we can help create a more supportive environment for everyone now and in the future.

Challenging Mental Health Stigma

Stigma is fueled by misunderstanding and fear, but it can be defeated through proper sources of information and open discussion. Here are a few ways we can assist in dismantling these barriers:

- **Start conversations**: Make mental health a regular topic of discussion in your home. This doesn't mean turning every mealtime into a therapy session but integrating mental wellness into everyday conversations with your children.
- **Model openness**: Show your willingness to talk about your feelings and personal challenges. When your children witness you openly sharing, it sets an example, making it easier for them to share their own struggles.
- **Correct misconceptions**: When you hear myths or stereotypes (or any misinformation) about mental health or therapy, gently correct them with facts. This could be in response to something said at home, seen on TV, or heard from friends.

Sharing Positive Experiences

People are more likely to consider therapy as a viable option for themselves when they hear about positive outcomes from someone they trust. Here's how sharing your journey can make a difference:

- **Personal stories**: If you or someone in your family has had a good experience with therapy, share that with others. Describe how it benefited you and what was involved, helping to demystify the process and make it less intimidating to them.
- **Success stories**: Collect and share stories of successful therapy experiences from people you know and from media resources. This could mean bringing up a news article or a podcast episode that sheds light on the benefits of therapy.

Educating About Mental Health

Education is a powerful tool for changing perceptions. It helps people to understand that mental health is just as important as physical health and that seeking professional help is a normal and positive step.

- **Use resources**: Countless resources are available to help educate yourself and others about mental health. Look for books, websites, and videos designed to explain mental health issues in convenient and accessible ways.
- **Host informal sessions**: Consider hosting a casual get-together or a virtual meet-up with friends and family to discuss mental health topics. Sometimes, a relaxed, laid-back setting can encourage more open conversation.

Role Models and Public Figures

When public figures and influencers speak openly about their mental health struggles and the benefits they've gained from therapy, it sends a powerful message. It shows people that pursuing professional help is not a weakness but a step towards healing and mental stability.

- **Highlight stories**: Share stories of celebrities or influencers who advocate for mental health awareness and have shared their therapy journeys. These stories can particularly impact teens and young adults who look up to these people.
- **Encourage local leaders**: In communities, local authorities, teachers, and coaches can play an important role in normalizing therapy. If you know any such individuals, encourage them to speak up about mental health.

As we work towards shifting the narrative around therapy and mental health, we help build a more compassionate and empathetic world. It's about creating spaces where everyone feels comfortable sharing their struggles and pursuing the support they need without fear of judgment. By challenging stigma, sharing our personal stories, educating ourselves and others, and looking up to those who lead by example, we contribute to a culture that prioritizes and values mental wellness.

In closing, remember that every conversation, every shared experience, and every piece of knowledge helps break down the barriers surrounding mental health care. Through these collaborative efforts, we can hope to see a future where therapy is as routine and unremarkable as visiting the dentist, a regular part of maintaining our overall well-being. As we move forward, let's embrace the understanding that mental health is an essential part of our lives, deserving of care, attention, and respect.

Embracing Empathy

As your reading journey comes to a close, I hope you feel much more confident about handling conflicts, disciplining your kids with a heart, and fostering open lines of communication in your home. Mehmet Oz once said that the opposite of anger wasn't calm, it was empathy, and I couldn't agree more. When you understand why you are angry and choose a path of self-soothing and positive conflict resolution, you exercise empathy not only toward others but also toward yourself. And this puts you in the perfect position to help someone else.

Before you go and try out the many strategies I have suggested, I hope you can do me one small favor. Please leave a sentence or two letting readers know what you thought of this book. It can do a world of good to a parent who would like to be in control of their anger, rather than the other way around.

Wishing you many moments of meaningful connection with your children, and the peace of mind that comes with using anger as a means to look within and make positive changes.

Scan the QR code to leave a review on Amazon.

CONCLUSION

This journey of anger management may seem challenging, but I promise you, there is light at the end of the tunnel. Navigating the often bumpy road of parenting with its sharp twists and turns of temper and the countless potholes of aggravation takes determination and grit. If there's one thing I hope you've picked up along this route (apart from an appreciation for my cliché analogies) it's that managing your anger is perfectly possible with the right tools, a sprinkle (or two) of humor, and a hefty dose of patience.

Remember, understanding your anger is like decoding a secret message from your brain. It's your body's way of saying, "Hey, something's not right here!" By recognizing the emotional and physical signs of anger we've discussed, you've taken a monumental first step toward managing that anger and understanding it on a deeper level—like a wise philosopher pondering the mysteries of the universe, or at least why socks go missing in the wash. (I'm still trying to figure that out myself.)

Empathy and communication are truly our guiding lights, illuminating the way to stronger family bonds. By understanding our emotions and those of our little ones (or not-so-little ones), we've discovered that the power of effective communication can effectively bridge gaps we once may have thought were impossible.

And let's not forget our tailored strategies for our children with diverse needs. Whether your child is neurodiverse or simply diverse in their ability to stir up mischief or create chaos from calm, we've discussed adaptable approaches that ensure you feel well-prepared. Like a parenting ninja, you'll be capable and ready to tackle any crisis with confidence and compassion.

Discipline without anger—ah, that can be a tricky one. We've revisited the art (or perhaps, the fine art) of setting boundaries and disciplining with love and patience instead of anger. We know that trying to discipline our children while blinded by rage only leads to fear, resentment, and hurt. When we discipline with love, we respect their dignity, increase their self-worth, and help them blossom into confident, emotionally healthy individuals.

And self-care? We've learned that self-care is not a luxury but a necessity. It serves as a crucial buffer against parental burnout. Neglecting our personal needs weakens our resolve, increases our stress, and leaves us utterly exhausted and overwhelmed. It's much easier to fly off the handle at the slightest injustice when we don't take care of ourselves. (Ask me how I know that.) Taking time to recharge and nurture ourselves not only benefits us mentally and physically but also helps us become better parents to our children. Never forget to prioritize self-care and make it a part of your daily routine! You deserve it!

Creating a family anger management plan is not just about finding a quick fix to our anger issues. It's about taking proactive steps towards building a harmonious home where peace reigns supreme (most of the time, anyway—let's be honest, we're not living in a cheesy made-for-TV movie from the 1970s).

And on a note that's close to my heart, we've talked about how seeking professional help when needed is a sign of strength and nothing to be ashamed of. It's about breaking the stigma around mental health support, wearing it like a badge of honor because, let's face it, it takes guts to ask for help.

I am living proof of the positive impact of pursuing professional help. I discovered a fantastic therapist and was diagnosed with anxiety and depression, both of which contributed to my anger issues. Through counseling and the proper medication, I gained better control of my emotions. Involving my family in therapy profoundly improved our lives, helping us to gain a deeper understanding and appreciation for one another. The therapy process greatly enhanced and strengthened our relationships.

In addition to therapy and the life-changing (and sanity-saving) blueprints outlined in this book, I gained the wisdom and assurance I needed to manage my anger while raising my children. By implementing these tools and strategies, along with plenty of trial and error (and the ability to laugh at myself), I slowly but steadily began to see progress. I was finally becoming the parent my children needed and deserved.

It wasn't always a walk in the park. As with any family, we still had our ups and downs. I found myself on the verge of blowing my top, more than I would like to admit. Thankfully, through self-discipline and perseverance, I was finally able to declare loudly and proudly that I had learned to conquer my anger issues. I was able to stay calm and redirect my emotions, even during times of turmoil. I had freed myself from anger's iron grasp. No more unhinged outbursts of fury or yelling at my kids. No more feelings of defeat. My household became one of peace and happiness, and my children flourished. I prevailed, and so can you!

So, as we part ways (for now), I invite you to view this not just as the end but as the beginning of a journey of continuous learning and growth in managing your anger. With commitment, understanding, and the strategies we've outlined, a peaceful, loving family dynamic isn't just a hopeful dream—it's a very achievable reality.

Here's to the journey ahead! May it be filled with love, laughter, and moments of peace amidst the beautiful chaos of raising children. May you always believe that the challenges of today can transform into the triumphs of tomorrow, guiding you to become the calm, composed parent you aspire to be. I have faith in you, and I know you've got this!

REFERENCES

1. Leonard, J. (n.d.). What to know about anger management for parents. Medical News Today. Retrieved from https://www.medicalnewstoday.com/articles/anger-management-for-parents
2. Parental stress and child mental health: A network analysis of... (n.d.). PMC. Retrieved from https://www.ncbi.nlm.nih.gov/pmc/articles/PMC9362691/
3. How to identify parenting triggers and 10 ways to deal with them. (n.d.). Times of India. Retrieved from https://timesofindia.indiatimes.com/readersblog/parenting-journey/how-to-identify-parenting-triggers-and-10-ways-to-deal-with-them-41867/
4. Breaking the Cycle of Anger: How DBT Techniques Can... (n.d.). New Milford Counseling Center. Retrieved from https://www.newmilfordcounselingcenter.com/blog/anger/breaking-the-cycle-of-anger-how-dbt-techniques-can-transform-your-life/
5. Here Is Why Everyone Should Have a Rage Journal. (n.d.). Blunt Therapy. Retrieved from https://www.blunt-therapy.com/rage-journal/
6. A Mindfulness Practice for Stressed-Out Parents. (n.d.). Mindful. Retrieved from https://www.mindful.org/when-parenting-gets-tough/
7. Adjusting Our Parenting Expectations. (n.d.). Aish. Retrieved from https://aish.com/adjusting-our-parenting-expectations/
8. Breathing to reduce stress. (n.d.). Better Health Channel. Retrieved from https://www.betterhealth.vic.gov.au/health/healthyliving/breathing-to-reduce-stress
9. Psychology Tools: How to Take a "Time Out". (n.d.). HealthyPsych. Retrieved from https://healthypsych.com/psychology-tools-how-to-take-a-time-out/
10. Positive Visualization: The Scientific Benefits Of Visualization. (n.d.). BetterHelp. Retrieved from https://www.betterhelp.com/advice/visualization/positive-visualization-the-scientific-benefits-of-visualization/
11. Managing Conflict with Humor. (n.d.). HelpGuide. Retrieved from https://www.helpguide.org/articles/relationships-communication/managing-conflicts-with-humor.htm
12. Active Listening. (n.d.). CDC. Retrieved from https://www.cdc.gov/parents/essentials/toddlersandpreschoolers/communication/activelistening.html
13. Nonverbal communication: body language and tone of voice. (n.d.). Raising Children Network. Retrieved from https://raisingchildren.net.au/toddlers/connecting-communicating/communicating/nonverbal-communication

14. Parental Roles: How to Set Healthy Boundaries with Your Child. (n.d.). Empowering Parents. Retrieved from https://www.empoweringparents.com/article/parental-roles-how-to-set-healthy-boundaries-with-your-child/

15. How to Apologize to Your Kids and Why It's Important. (n.d.). Parents. Retrieved from https://www.parents.com/parenting/better-parenting/advice/how-to-apologize-to-your-kids-the-right-way/

16. Managing anger: ideas for parents. (n.d.). Raising Children Network. Retrieved from https://raisingchildren.net.au/guides/first-1000-days/looking-after-yourself/anger-management-for-parents

17. Essential Lesson Plans for Emotional Regulation Skills. (n.d.). Everyday Speech. Retrieved from https://everydayspeech.com/blog-posts/general/creating-calm-essential-lesson-plans-for-emotional-regulation-skills/

18. The Safe Place: An Essential Tool for Kids' Emotional Growth. (n.d.). Richland First Steps. Retrieved from https://richlandfirststeps.org/safe-place-essential-tools-kids-emotional-growth/

19. 10 Tips for Successful Family Meetings - 10.249. (n.d.). Colorado State University Extension. Retrieved from https://extension.colostate.edu/topic-areas/family-home-consumer/10-tips-for-successful-family-meetings/

20. How To Improve Communication With Your Neurodivergent Child. (n.d.). Affinity Psychology. Retrieved from https://affinitypsych.com/how-to-improve-communication-with-your-neurodivergent-child/

21. BrainyQuote. "Anger Quotes." Accessed June 18, 2024. https://www.brainyquote.com/topics/anger-quotes